MW00989337
HOME
TEACHING
WITH PURPOSE AND POWER

Home Teaching
with Purpose and Power

Richard J. Marshall

Deseret Book Company
Salt Lake City, Utah

Dedicated to the priesthood quorums
of the University Ninth Ward
for six remarkable years of home teaching

Library of Congress Cataloging-in-Publication Data

Marshall, Richard (Richard James)
Home teaching with purpose and power / by Richard Marshall.
p. cm.
Includes bibliographical references and index.
ISBN 0-87579-371-1
1. Family—Religious life. 2. Christian education—Home training. 3. Visitations in Christian education. 4. Church of Jesus Christ of Latter-day Saints—Education. 5. Mormon Church—Education.
I. Title.
BX8643.F3M35 1990
268'.432—dc20 90-41525
CIP

Printed in the United States of America

10 9 8 7 6 5 4

"There is no greater Church calling than that of a home teacher. There is no greater Church service rendered to our Father in Heaven's children than the service rendered by a humble, dedicated, committed home teacher."

President Ezra Taft Benson
Ensign, May 1987, p. 48

Contents

1

Confessions of a Halfhearted Home Teacher

The red car accelerated up the ramp and onto the freeway, and the two men inside settled back comfortably, pleased to be heading out of the city so early in the morning. They had already spent some pleasant minutes conversing together as they had worked their way across town.

"You're serious? You really want me to tell you what's wrong with the Church's home teaching program?" The speaker laughed warmly as he asked the question. An aggressive and successful company manager during business hours, he was driving toward a waiting golf course two hours away. His voice was charged with good humor. There was plenty of time—they had the entire sun-filled Saturday to themselves. His companion was his own father-in-law, a close friend, a bracing conversationalist, and a man of considerable Church experience.

"Your wife—my daughter—says she continues to be genuinely proud of your progress since you joined the Church, but lately she's become concerned that you haven't accepted your home teaching assignments with your usual enthusiasm. In fact, she says you're 'dying on the vine.' She also says you are becoming very vocal about your negative feelings."

The younger man chuckled again. "My wife—your daughter—knows perfectly well that I joined the Church so I could marry her, and that even though I did the right thing for the wrong reasons, I have since become totally, gloriously converted to the gospel. I know it is true." He mused a moment, reflecting on those early months of marriage, difficult times of adjustment to Mormon membership and its immediate culture shock. "And I'm quite willing to admit that at first it wasn't easy," he added. "Tithing was hard, three meetings every Sunday were overwhelming, and plunging into the Mormon activities whirlwind would have been quite beyond me if it hadn't been for her. Sally did a great job of making me feel at home in our ward, helping me learn to roll with the punches. I have come to enjoy it all—all but home teaching. Home teaching is different. Home teaching is a real problem for me, a thorn in my side—and it's getting worse."

He paused again and made his point a second time, muttering, "It certainly isn't getting any better. Home teaching is like pain. I forget how terrible it is until I have to go through it again." There was no smile now. Humor had drained from his voice.

"I'm surprised to hear that, Fred," the older man said, holding back his own thoughts, the silence forcing the son-in-law to continue his complaint.

"Well, I'm just as sorry to say it, because home teaching wasn't a bore and a burden that first year. I suspect it was because they sent me out with an accomplished companion. He had been in the bishopric, knew everybody, handled the whole thing. I just sat there and looked agreeable during our visits. But if we had a purpose in going, I certainly wasn't aware of it. We did no teaching, as I recall. He did all the talking.

"But now it's different." Fred sighed. "Now I'm the senior companion, the new Melchizedek Priesthood holder. Now I'm in charge, and it just isn't working out. I don't enjoy home teaching, so I put it off until the end of the month. Usually we have a lot of fumbling around before we get together, and then we can't find our families home. When we do find them, our visit isn't very uplifting or entertaining. It's painful for them; it's painful for me. As a result, I have little or nothing to report when my quorum leader lays on me one of those quick, catch-as-catch-can evaluation interviews. Frankly, they embarrass me. The whole thing distresses me, and I just don't want to continue. That's what I told Sally, that I'm going to ask the bishop to release me as a home teacher—so called."

The older man actually laughed. "Is that all? Nothing more?"

His laughter was infectious. The driver smiled again and said, "Sure, there's more. And since you've brought up the subject—and I'm sure your daughter put you up to it and made sure we'd have all day to gnaw on it together—let me also add that I haven't treated this lightly. I've been agonizing over my miserable attitude. I don't want home teaching to turn me sour on other programs within the Church—programs that really are inspired. So I've been searching for answers. I've analyzed my home teaching problem just as I would break down a problem at the office, just like the exercises we used to go through while I was getting my MBA. And I've come up with four basic areas that make home teaching most unpleasant for me, and perhaps for everyone else."

"Only four?"

Fred caught the humor and glanced sideways at his father-in-law but pressed on. "Only four errors in home teaching as our ward does it, but they are four big difficulties for me. Let me name them in order," and he held up the index finger on his right hand. "First, I am assigned five families without any notice. I am literally thrust upon them without any previous counsel or consideration. I learn about them from my priesthood leader, who catches me after church in the parking lot. He waits while I write down the five names, but I can learn very little about them from him because he does not really know them either. When I do meet the five families, I discover we have almost nothing in common. One family quite openly does not want any home teachers, especially me, a complete stranger and a convert. They are inactive and merely tolerate my visits. I cannot warm them up to me. I can see no value in even going into their home." Then he added, "Frankly, I can see no purpose in going to the other four homes."

And he held up two fingers on his right hand. "Second, I am requested during these parking-lot instructions to take a young Aaronic Priesthood holder with me. We also do not know each other, but I soon discover that he is very busy with high school activities and almost never available. He does not return my phone calls. When we do get together, it is obvious he would rather be elsewhere. He and I have even less in common than the families we teach. At least the parents are fellow adults and stay home some nights."

When Fred held three fingers up, the father-in-law smiled, for it looked identical to the Boy Scout sign. This reluctant home teacher had never been a Boy Scout. He missed the humor of it entirely.

"Third, no one has ever really explained to me what I am supposed to accomplish by all these monthly visits. What should I teach? What should I say? How should I use my junior companion? How can I, a newcomer to Mormonism, a rank outsider in many ways, teach anything these longtime member families have not already heard? And am I really supposed to be checking up on their family prayers and asking them point blank if they're getting along together? Who am I to intrude on their personal lives? If I ask them questions like these, I seem to be prying, playing the sinister investigator. Thus far, our home teaching visits—and usually I go alone or with Sally—have proven worthless. I've tried it for seven months now, and I'm tired of it all.

"Finally," and Fred waved a full four fingers toward his father-in-law, "number four on my list of unpleasant home teaching areas is this unceasing pressure for me to get into those five homes at any cost. When I was sent out of town once and missed all five families, why, my quorum president made me feel as bad as if I'd just committed adultery! I've learned that 100 percent is vital because 100 percent is perfection, and perfection is what we Mormons are working for in life. With home teaching, I gain instant perfection monthly!" he scoffed. "Which Church president said, 'Every member a statistic'?"

"It was David O. McKay," the older man said dryly. "And what he said was, 'Every member a missionary.' But go on. I'm listening."

"So—I must be prepared to report on the status of each family at the end of the month. What status? Am I there to teach them something? Am I really representing Christ? Or am I supposed to be sniffing out internal family difficulties I can pass along to random line leaders in the ward parking lot, or in a crowded hall between meetings? Because that's where most of my personal priesthood interviews take place." This was cynically said, but he softened his tone as he murmured, "Frankly, I resent it all."

They drove on in heavy silence for several minutes before the older man spoke.

"You're sure that's all? Just the four unpleasant areas?"

The driver stole another sideways look at his father-in-law, noting he was smiling broadly, and his own firm face immediately melted. But they both knew it had been a well-constructed indictment. Because the older man still held back, Fred continued.

"Soooo," and he cleared his throat, "you've got to admit I make a strong point or two—or four. And it seems to me that the question I have to ask is a very simple one: Is the LDS home teaching program really inspired? commanded of God? And if it is, why do I feel so miserable about it?" Another pause followed. "And the burden of proof, dear father-in-law, is yours." He reached over and patted him on the knee for emphasis. "Because," and he sighed again, "there's no inspiration in what I've been assigned to do. So let's hear from you now."

The white-haired man put his hands behind his head, lacing his fingers, stretching, smiling.

"You know, Freddy, your problems with home teaching carry me back to problems of my own during the early 1960s, right after correlation was presented to the Church. Someone came up with the idea that the priesthood bearers should carry a specific message to their families each month—a message that was probably thought up by some well-meaning committee at Church headquarters. These messages were printed on little slips of paper. Not a bad idea.

"But after a few years, the teaching ideas for the little messages wore pretty thin." He chuckled to himself, remembering. "They gave every set of home teachers a green book each year to record the family names and other information, and in the back of the book were the twelve monthly messages. We discussed the new message each month with the family, and after the visit, we tore out the printed slip and left it with them. The reason I'm amused in thinking about this is that the committee started running out of good ideas for messages—and we ended up with some really weak ones, really strange ones. Many had absolutely no application for some of our families.

"I vividly recall standing on the front porch of a house where Tom and I—we were both young elders—had never found the father at home, only the mother with four bright little children. We were very dutiful in giving the proper message from the green home teaching book, elaborating on it as required." He savored the memory flooding back. "So just before he knocked, Tom held up the slip, showed it to me, and suggested that it was my turn to teach the family. The printed message was on communism—and he obviously didn't want to give it to all those little children, who simply wouldn't understand it. He then claimed he had given last month's message, the one on safe driving. No, no, I objected, I had given last month's message, and it wasn't on safe driving; it was on profanity. I remembered giving it well—for none of those little children even knew what profanity was! Well, Tom finally agreed with me, and his shoulders sagged as he took the message slip back.

"We were welcomed inside, and he spent the next few minutes reading from the slip and convincing the children that communism was a blight on the world. We hoped they were uplifted by all this. We had a pleasant exchange with the mother on how the family was doing, I gave a nice closing prayer, and we said good-bye. But just as we walked off the porch, Tom heard the oldest child ask his mother softly, 'Mama, what is communism?' "

"And that's the point I'm making," Fred erupted. "Where is the inspiration in teaching little children about communism and safe driving?"

"But don't you see? That is an important part of the divine plan," the father-in-law said patiently. "We are mere mortals striving to implement a program the Lord has commanded us to carry out. But he doesn't tell us exactly how to do it! That's always been the challenge to Church leaders, to figure out the best way to accomplish what the Lord requires. We may stumble around trying to produce a plan for home teaching, but the idea for visiting every member at home is already perfect. It was commanded by God." And he bent forward and searched through the briefcase at his feet. He pulled out a book and quickly opened it. "See, God gives the basic commandment to home teach, but he then says, let's see—yes, right here: 'For behold, it is not meet that I should command in all things; for he that is compelled in all things, the same is a slothful and not a wise servant.' "[1] He leaned toward Fred, holding up the book, his finger still touching the scripture he had read.

"So God is commanding us to home teach, but he isn't going to tell us exactly what we should say each visit," the father-in-law said, stabbing the page for emphasis. "And did you note that God interchanges the word 'compelled' with 'commanded.' When we are commanded to home teach, we are also compelled to home teach."

"Yes, but I haven't yet heard the words 'home teach' anywhere in the scriptures," returned the driver. "Read me where it says 'home teaching' in the Doctrine and Covenants."

"Easily done," replied his father-in-law, and he quickly turned a few pages in the book. "In the very first month the Church was organized, in April of 1830, the Lord revealed to Joseph Smith the essence of home teaching: 'To watch over the church always, and be with and strengthen them; and see that there is no iniquity in the church . . . and see that the church meet together often, and also see that all the members do their duty.'[2]

"And in that same revelation," the older man continued, "the Lord explained how this Church-wide strengthening would be accomplished. For he also commanded—and this is the key—'And visit the house of each member, exhorting them to pray vocally and in secret and attend to all family duties.'[3] We must recognize that Joseph Smith—great as he was—couldn't visit the home of each member of the Church—small as it was then. Even the most dedicated bishop can't do that now. That's God's commission to all priesthood holders. That's home teaching! And there isn't another so-called Christian church in all the world that makes any attempt to do this astonishing thing: to watch over every family and individual in the entire church on at least a monthly basis." The older man had greatly warmed to his subject, and he leaned closer as he climaxed his explanation.

"Home teaching," he said slowly, "is one of the singular signs of the true church."

The reluctant home teacher frowned. "But those weak messages about communism and—"

"Oh, fiddle!" retorted the father-in-law. "Don't you see? Home teaching is the vehicle to get priesthood visitors into every home on a continuous basis, to 'watch over the church always,' as the Lord said. Overcoming weak messages, that's an obvious need—but that occurs after you've determined to go visit your families, to sit with them in their homes. In those first correlation years, they may have had some messages that didn't apply to everyone—not to children—but at least the vehicle was working. Tom and I were there! We represented the Lord to that little family. If we confused them with communism, at least we also inquired about their welfare, we looked around and saw that everything seemed all right, and we left a priesthood blessing in the home. That's worth everything. And they knew we cared about them. After all, we had set aside some time just for them. They had to have felt they were important to us."

"Hmmm," mused Fred, taking one hand from the wheel to stroke his chin meditatively. "Then you're saying the specific message isn't really as important as being in someone's home monthly?"

"No, I'm saying there are some marvelously uplifting messages that priesthood holders should be bringing into their assigned homes. But first they've got to be there. I'm also saying that when men try to implement and articulate a commandment of God, they may have to shift about a little until they find out how to do it." He patted the book in his lap.

"The Lord doesn't give Church leaders all the answers, nor even individual home teachers. But he does say he wants us to be 'anxiously engaged in a good cause,'[4] and that's what today's home teaching is all about, trying to figure out what's good for each family, for each individual."

The driver squinted down the road, contemplating. "So you're saying home teaching is a divinely inspired vehicle we have to drive into every member's home, but that we also have to figure out for ourselves what message we should be carrying in the vehicle—and how it should be unloaded?"

"Exactly," replied the father-in-law. "And very colorfully stated. The Lord wants home teachers to figure out what's best for each individual family. That's because everyone has a different set of needs. It's also an important part of another Church-wide emphasis called 'perfecting the Saints.' "

"And the LDS Church has had home teaching—in one form or another—since the beginning? Since, what was it, 1830?" Fred inquired.

"Home teaching is a latter-day commandment, yes," replied the father-in-law. "But remember, home teaching has always been a basic gospel function. That being true, then there has always been some considerable energy spent on home teaching wherever the Lord's church existed."

"Since joining the Church," the young man said, "I've learned that Adam had the gospel. Would you think he also sent out home teachers?" He asked this facetiously, but the reply was immediate.

"Certainly. As with every father, Adam was commanded to watch over his family—which was the entire human race in those days—and when it grew beyond his ability to visit the home of each family member, he had to find a way to accomplish that inspired task."

"Ahhh, you have chapter and verse on that?"asked Fred with a sly smile.

"Surely," replied his passenger. "Let me find it in the book of Moses here." And he bent to the task. "Ah, yes, listen to this: 'Adam and Eve blessed the name of God, and they made all things known unto their sons and their daughters.'[5] And here again," he read. " 'And thus the Gospel began to be preached, from the beginning. . . . And thus all things were confirmed unto Adam, by an holy ordinance, and the Gospel preached, and a decree sent forth, that it should be in the world.' "[6] The father-in-law looked up. "And how could a decree be sent forth except someone be sent to all the children's homes? Someone assigned by Adam. That's home teaching in ancient times," he said with finality.

"Okay, but—"

"One more from the book of Moses," interrupted the father-in-law. "This is God counseling Adam: 'Therefore I give unto you a commandment, to teach these things freely unto your children.' "[7]

Fred had always been amazed over his father-in-law's gift at finding scriptures. "And I suppose you can also find home teaching in the New Testament?"

His passenger bent down again, brought forth still another book, and said, "Glad you asked. This one is easy to find. Listen to what the Apostle James says when he describes the flawless exercise of religion: 'Pure religion and undefiled before God and the Father is this, to visit the fatherless and widows in their affliction.'[8] Now, if that isn't what Tom and I were doing for that mother alone with her four children, I don't know what is."

The older man gazed at the countryside sweeping by them and reflected, "And I suppose that even though Tom presented a somewhat inept message to that little family that day, yet, if they had been in serious want, we would have recognized it—and helped them. That's pure religion. That's why we were there. That's what we were doing."

He turned again to the first book he had laid in his lap. "Now let me give you the benefit of the wisdom of old King Benjamin from the Book of Mormon." He flipped through the pages, found the verse, placed his finger on the words, and looked at his companion.

"You'll recall that this king is also a very humble prophet to the Nephites. When he is tired and old and ready to die, he calls together all of the families of his kingdom—which would be the entire Church—for he wishes to give them the sum total, the essence, of all that he has learned about life and what it means to properly serve the Lord. He has a communications problem, as it says here, 'For the multitude being so great that King Benjamin could not teach them all . . . therefore he caused a tower to be erected, that thereby his people might hear the words which he should speak unto them.'[9]

"And what is the greatest single message he could deliver just before he dies? What is the capstone lesson he could teach to these families as their father figure, the consummate home teacher? He gives to them the superlative key to successful living. He says to them: 'I tell you these things that ye may learn wisdom; that ye may learn that when ye are in the service of your fellow beings ye are only in the service of your God.'[10] He is telling them exactly what James said, that service to others is pure religion.

"That's the way King Benjamin and James put it in their day. And in our day we call it—hang onto your hat, my boy—home teaching."

Sally's husband narrowed his eyes, studying the highway stretched out ahead of his speeding red car. He loved his wife for her constant concern for him. She was a great companion, and he loved her for what she had done this day, setting her father up to give him a mighty shot in the arm regarding his miserable feelings as a home teacher. Finally he spoke.

"I give up. I guess you're right. Home teaching is an inspired program."

"You guess I'm right?" The older man whooped.

"Okay, okay. *You are right.* Home teaching was commanded of God in all ages, and instructions can be inspired even in a parking lot." He paused to weigh his next words. "But if home teaching has the divine touch—then why do I feel so rotten about it?"

His father-in-law leaned over and slapped him affectionately on the back. "Why? Because, regardless of your MBA and all your good intentions, you haven't yet learned that if you want to harvest corn, then you must *plant* corn!"

Notes

1. D&C 58:26.
2. D&C 20:53–55.
3. D&C 20:51.
4. D&C 58:27.
5. Moses 5:12.
6. Moses 5:58–59.
7. Moses 6:58.
8. James 1:27.
9. Mosiah 2:7.
10. Mosiah 2:17.

2

A Halfhearted Home Teacher Repents

The red car continued swiftly down the freeway, but inside was consternation and concern.

"Plant corn? *Plant corn?* Now wait a minute! If you're saying I must sprinkle seeds of friendship in those homes if I want a friendly response from each family—if you're saying I have to plan better meetings so—!"

The father-in-law cut Fred's harangue short merely by holding up his hand. With feigned benevolence he declared, "From what you've told me, you don't really seem to understand what to do once you and your companion are inside the home, or that you need considerable preparation before you even get there. You seem adrift. You'll appreciate this old Chinese saying: 'If you don't know where you're going—then you're on your way.' "

The Chinese saying did not erase Fred's frown. "And Sally wants you to teach me how to home teach on our golfing day?"

"Look, if I have an advantage over you, it's not in golf—it's in priesthood experience. If I could offer some suggestions that might make your home teaching—" But now he stopped in midsentence as his son-in-law's hand went up.

"And I thank you for your kind offer to help me," the younger man said pleasantly enough. "But you did not hear me a minute ago. I said I want *out!* I am still going to insist that the bishop release me as a home teacher."

"But didn't you just agree it was an inspired program?"

"True enough—inspired for others, but not for me." Fred glanced sideways at his father-in-law. "The Church has many callings. No person fits them all. Not everyone can lead the choir, conduct a sacrament service, or balance the ward budget." He paused for emphasis. "And not everyone fits the mold of a home teacher. I'm one of those. I don't fit the mold—and I don't want to continue going pointlessly into those homes anymore!" The older man shut his eyes tight and made a terrible grimace. He held it for his companion to see.

"I know, I know," was the young man's response. "And I get the feeling you're not going to give up, keeping your teeth clamped on my leg all day." He laughed to relieve the other. "Look, you're more than my father-in-law. You're a true friend. But you also remind me of the senior officer who interviewed me just before I was supposed to be released from the Navy. He tried every possible argument to get me to re-enlist. I was determined not to. I finally told him that even if they made me an admiral and gave me a fleet to command with Miss America as my adjutant, I still would not re-enlist. I thought that I'd finally made my point, because he shrugged, wrote a notation on my personal file, and dismissed me.

"But as I walked past him, I glanced at what he had written. In the space marked 'Re-enlistment Plans,' he had neatly printed: 'Undecided.' "

The father-in-law remained silent.

"Look, you have a convincing argument that home teaching is the will of the Lord," the young man continued. "It existed from Adam's day down to the Apostle James and was lauded by good King Benjamin on his tower, yet I still don't want to do it!" A little vexation had crept into the younger man's voice. "It is all too new to me. I've been an outsider for most of my life. I'm still learning. I have nothing to teach anyone—let alone those five families who are stuck with me. And most of all, I'm just plain uncomfortable trying to posture as an inspired home teacher. I want out!"

The father-in-law reflected as the red car flew past a herd of grazing dairy cows. "Your talk about being an outsider stirs my memory," he said. "In the early history of the Church, everyone who joined was an outsider. Yet, unproven men like Parley Pratt and Wilford Woodruff were baptized, ordained, and called on missions within a handful of days, and they were great, productive missionaries."

"I'm no Parley Pratt."

"All right, that does it," exclaimed the father-in-law in a cheery voice. He bent down and rustled through his briefcase once again. "I didn't think I'd have to refer to this, but you've pushed me too far with your argument about being 'new' and being an 'outsider.' So when Sally said home teaching was your very big problem, I brought along my home teaching file, little things I've collected over the years."

He thumbed through several publications and peered at one. "Yes, this is it." He waved several pages at Fred. "Now, listen to this. It's a treasure—a historic statement of William Cahoon, who joined the Church October 16, 1830, just six and a half months after the revelation setting forth home teaching responsibilities—the 20th section of the Doctrine and Covenants, which I quoted earlier. Let me read young Cahoon to you: 'I was called and ordained to act as a ward teacher to visit the families of the saints. I got along very well 'till I found that I was obliged to pay a visit to the Prophet. Being young, only about 17 years of age, I felt my weakness in visiting the Prophet and his family in the capacity of a teacher. I almost felt like shrinking from duty.

Finally, I went to his door and knocked, and in a minute the Prophet came to the door. I stood there trembling and said to him, "Brother Joseph, I have come to visit you in the capacity of a ward teacher, if it is convenient for you." He said, "Brother William, come right in; I am glad to see you, sit down in that chair there, and I will go call my family in."

" 'They soon came in and took seats. He then said, "Brother William, I submit myself and family into your hands," and took his seat. "Now, Brother William," he said, "ask all the questions you feel like."

" 'By this time my fears and trembling had ceased, and I said, "Brother Joseph, are you trying to live your religion?"

" 'He answered, "Yes."

" 'Then I said, "Do you pray in your family?"

" 'He said, "Yes."

" ' "Do you teach your family the principles of the gospel?"

" 'He replied, "Yes, I am trying to do it."

" ' "Do you ask a blessing on your food?"

" 'He answered, "Yes."

" ' "Are you trying to live in peace and harmony with all your family?"

" 'He said that he was.

" 'I turned to Sister Emma, his wife, and said, "Sister Emma, are you trying to live your religion? Do you teach your children to obey their parents? Do you try to teach them to pray?"

" 'To all these questions, she answered, "Yes, I am trying to do so."

" 'I then turned to Joseph and said, "I am now through with my questions as a teacher; and now if you have any instructions to give, I shall be happy to receive them."

" 'He said, "God bless you, Brother William; and if you are humble and faithful, you shall have power to settle all difficulties that may come before you in the capacity of a teacher."

" 'I then left my parting blessing upon him and his family, as a teacher, and took my departure.' "[1]

The father-in-law laid the pages in his lap, looked at Fred, and said, "Isn't that a remarkable statement? A brand-new convert, just seventeen years old, and he marches right into the home of the Prophet himself, all alone, and puts Joseph's feet to the fire, does the job, leaves a blessing, and goes on his way with an indelible experience we can still read about today, over 160 years later."

Fred gripped the wheel and gritted his teeth.

"So you want out of home teaching because you're an outsider?" the father-in-law asked rhetorically. "That teen-age boy had just joined the Church. But he was fulfilling a priesthood assignment as best he could."

He rifled through more papers. "Now let's talk about the age spectrum for home teachers. If William Cahoon was only seventeen, what about old men? What is the cut-off age for home teachers? Let me read you a quotation from Joseph F. Smith, who was president of the Church when he made this statement in 1914: 'We have had called to our attention, recently, the fact that some men who are of long standing in the Church—indeed, some of them born and reared in the Church, and who are occupying prominent positions in some of the quorums of the priesthood—when their presidents or their bishops of the wards in which they live call upon them to visit the Saints, teach the principles of the Gospel and perform the duties of teachers, they coolly inform their bishops that they have graduated from that calling, and refuse to act as teachers. Brother Charles W. Penrose [an apostle] is eighty-two years of age. I am going on seventy-six, and I believe that I am older than several of these good men who have graduated from the duties in the Lesser Priesthood, and I want to tell them and you that we are not too old to act as teachers, if you will call us to do it—not one of us. There is never a time, there never will come a time to those who hold the priesthood in the Church of Jesus Christ of Latter-day Saints, when men can say of themselves that they have done enough. So long as life lasts, and so long as we possess ability to do good, to labor for the upbuilding of Zion and for the benefit of the human family, we ought, with willingness, to yield with alacrity to the requirements made of us to do our duty, little or great.' "[2]

" 'So long as life lasts'?" asked the bemused driver. "Priesthood holders never ask to be released from home teaching?"

"Never." His passenger replied in a voice of pretended harshness but then laughed easily. "So I've just read you a Church president saying that age doesn't matter, and that even busy apostles will serve as home teachers if called. But that's a pretty big 'if.' I mean, who is going to call a busy apostle to be a home teacher to three or four neighborhood families?"

"Who indeed?" echoed the son-in-law.

"May I share with you, then, a most remarkable exhibition of home teaching, one that I personally witnessed?" And without waiting for an answer, the passenger continued. "This occurred just before general conference during a Regional Representatives' meeting in the Church Office Building auditorium in Salt Lake City, with all the General Authorities and auxiliary leaders joining in." He paused. "I'm guessing it was around 1975 or 1976. The Presiding Bishop, Victor L. Brown, was talking about the importance of properly involving the Aaronic Priesthood young men as companions in home teaching. As an important feature in his demonstration, he called up a young teachers quorum president, a boy who had been sitting totally unnoticed on the front row facing the stage, sitting there beside the First Presidency and Council of the Twelve.

"Bishop Brown asked the boy his name, his ward and stake, and so forth, while standing before the microphone with his arm comfortingly around him. And then he queried him about his home teaching assignment. Did he have one? Yes. Did he get out every month? Yes, every month. Did he enjoy home teaching? You bet. What was his Melchizedek Priesthood holder companion like? A wonderful person, the boy said. Did they ever prepare their lessons before going out? Yes, every time, and days in advance. Was he personally assigned something to do with the families? Always."

The father-in-law's face filled with pleasure. He was reliving a sterling moment among his memories.

"Finally, he asked the boy—addressing him as 'president,' honoring the fact that he presided over his small quorum of teachers—he asked him how he felt, personally felt, about his senior partner in all of this. The youth, standing tall and straight for all his fifteen years, standing bravely in front of this intimidating assemblage, said that his home teaching companion was the finest man he had ever known—next to his own father. He admired him; he loved teaching with him; he had learned much from him. 'And is he with us here today?' the bishop asked. Yes, he is here. 'And will you please go bring him up here—to join us in front of this marvelous group of priesthood leaders?' Yes, the boy would do that.

"He stepped down off the low podium, stepped one pace down, right in front of the First Presidency, and took the waiting hand of a smiling N. Eldon Tanner, first counselor to President Spencer W. Kimball."

"Good heavens!" exclaimed the surprised driver.

"Good heavens is right," replied his father-in-law. "The perfect exclamation. God is in his heavens and all is well with the world because even today's busy apostles can find time to home teach—just as President Joseph F. Smith suggested so many years ago." He reached over, patting his son-in-law on the shoulder. "And is there a big message in all of that for you?"

"Okay, you've made me say uncle! I'll have to give up. You win. I won't ask to be released. But it becomes obvious that I have missed something very necessary in preparing myself as a home teacher—or somebody somewhere should have given me some training and confidence I don't now have." He sighed audibly. "Obviously neither you nor Sally is going to let me just fade away and quit." His face then became awash with the relaxed grin he had worn earlier when they were just leaving the city. "So now that you've beaten me up about not being a conscientious home teacher, you've got to give me some suggestions about how to do it, how to improve my performance." He stole a look at his passenger and added, "And stifle my ugly attitude."

"Not to worry," the pleased father-in-law said. "For we have many more miles to travel and thirty-six holes of golf to play. I've got a head full of proven home teaching ideas you might enjoy hearing and chewing on."

He leaned over the papers in his lap, returning them to the file in the briefcase at his feet. He paused, peered down, then looked over at his son-in-law once again.

"But before I put this stuff away, let me show you the most famous home teacher today—uh, in my judgment. You might be amused at this." And he held up a sheaf of pages stapled together. "See, here is his picture on the cover of *Time* magazine. I clipped it and his cover story years ago—forgot I'd put them in this home teaching file. Let me read the introduction to you." The father-in-law adjusted his glasses, holding the pages comfortably before him.

"The man featured in this magazine story is Jack Anderson, the syndicated columnist who has long been known—as it says right here—as the 'pre-eminent scourge of Washington D.C.' " And he commenced reading: " 'When Washington correspondent Hays Gorey began calling on Jack Anderson to interview him for this week's cover story in the Press section, there was no need to get acquainted. They first met 25 years ago when both were young newsmen for the Salt Lake City Tribune. Their contact then was slight, but, says Gorey, "When I came to Washington for TIME in 1965, the first telephone call I got was from Jack Anderson. He had heard—he hears everything—that I had arrived, and he wanted to take me to lunch."

" 'They met frequently after that when Anderson made hour-long monthly visits to the Gorey household. He came not to talk politics or scandal, but religion. Anderson is a lay teacher for the Mormon Church, responsible for keeping in touch with a number of Mormons in the neighborhood, and Mrs. Gorey is one of them.' "[3]

"Good heavens again!" gushed the son-in-law.

The older man laid the magazine article in his lap and mused out loud: "Now, isn't that a marvelous thing for Jack Anderson?"

"A marvelous thing?"

"Why, yes. Hear it again," and the father-in-law lifted up the pages and read: " 'Anderson is a lay teacher for the Mormon Church, responsible for keeping in touch with a number of Mormons in the neighborhood.' See, Jack Anderson has been doing exactly what the Lord commanded back in 1830: he's been watching over the Church by visiting the homes of his assigned families. He's been responsive to his stewardship as a home teacher. Those families know that; his bishop knows that; the recording angels know that; and now millions of *Time* magazine readers also know that. Jack Anderson is a dutiful home teacher."

Notes

1. *Juvenile Instructor*, 27:493.
2. *Conference Report*, April 1914, p. 7.
3. *Time*, April 3, 1972, p. 40.

3

Being There – The Most Important Thing in Home Teaching

Leaving the red car rushing onward toward the golf course, the scene now shifts from Saturday to Sunday, from the great outdoors to the spacious interior of a crowded LDS chapel filled wall to wall with eager faces. The doors to the cultural hall were pulled apart and more chairs set up to accommodate the overflowing congregation. The meeting was a stake conference in a major metropolis on the east coast of the United States.

A well-rehearsed choir sat behind the speaker. Flowers festooned the stand. The entire congregation had just sat down, having sung an exhilarating hymn. The new stake president was at the pulpit, just getting into his talk: "I don't suppose any of you were more surprised to see me called as president of this great stake than I was." A spattering of laughter followed this remark, for everyone admired the speaker. "I enjoyed being bishop these past five years, perhaps the greatest five years of my life." He looked fondly down at the front row where his beaming family was seated.

"I frankly thought that when I was released as bishop, I'd go from 'who's who' to 'who's he?' " More light-hearted laughter came from the congregation, for he had gladdened and charmed them all as a high councilor. His spirituality and eagerness to help had made him popular and welcome throughout the stake.

"But for my first address as stake president, I would like to speak out on what I believe to be one of the most important programs in the Church—and perhaps the least appreciated by many of us sitting right here today." He paused, looked about, and measured his audience once more.

"I'm talking about home teaching, high-quality home teaching, the kind that encourages, inspires, and lifts the hearts and minds of all of us, the weak and the wayward, the strong and the stout. I'm talking about home teaching that is motivated by only one quality: the pure love of Christ—home teaching with no other incentive than just to be there, in the home of friends you've made, helping parents, encouraging their children. It doesn't matter if someone is married or not, has children or not. An individual living alone constitutes a family unit in the eyes of the Lord—yes, and in the eyes of his church.

"I'm talking about home teaching that has no reward other than the shared fellowship and enduring faithfulness that, as the Lord has said, 'is stronger than the cords of death.'[1]

"President Harold B. Lee once said, 'Home teaching is the instrument by which we see to it, through the priesthood, that every program in the Church is made available to parents and their children.'[2]

"So I would like to tell you a true story that happened right here among us, a story that illustrates what President Lee said." The speaker looked again across his entire congregation, from the sunlit chapel back to the distant and dim figures sitting in the obscurity of the cultural hall stage.

"It is the story of a stranger who came into our midst many years ago, came here to this great city seeking employment, came here from having been raised virtually in the shadows of the temple back in Utah. But Bob—let us call him Bob—had another reason for venturing this far from his home: he wanted to put as much distance between himself and the LDS Church as possible.

"Bob's bitterness involved a number of problems. He had fallen into bad habits as a teenager. His not living the Word of Wisdom alienated him from some of his friends. His inactivity in his ward had become a source of antagonism between him and his family. The new friends he made helped feed his rancor. They convinced each other that the Mormon Church so dominated their community that they would never find the kind of freedom they desired in such a 'smothering environment.' Bob's mind began soaking up this animosity, sopping up all its bitter juices. And about the time his high school classmates were being called on missions, Bob decided he would also leave town, leave to go away to college and never return.

"But the university he chose was in a nearby state, and there were still plenty of Mormons on campus. The Church influence seemed to be everywhere. So when he married a nonmember girl, she had already agreed with him that they should get as far away as possible to build their life and rear their children. And so they came to this great city—where they could lose themselves from their former lives—with hardly a word to family or friends as to exactly where they were going."

The stake president had given many a talk in his day. He was easy to listen to. He was a storyteller. He loved to quote the scriptures. His speaking stance was to grasp both sides of the rostrum, lean slightly forward, and look directly out into the faces of his listeners. He released his hold only to leaf through the Standard Works or to make a powerful gesture. But there were no scriptures now as he continued his story of the elusive, recalcitrant Bob, the stumbling soul from Utah who had purposefully lost his way and fled to the metropolis.

"Bob and his wife both found work here and rented a

little apartment, and life for them settled into a quiet routine for half a year. If they missed their families in the West, they were too caught up in the excitement of their new marriage, their new employment, the big-city horizons.

"And then one night, just after they had eaten a simple meal and were settled back in their rented furniture, there came a knock at the door. Who could that possibly be? They knew almost no one in their building, and no one at all in the neighborhood. It was the wife who answered the door while Bob, newspaper in hand, paused to listen.

" 'Excuse me, Madam,' a stranger said in a voice heavy with a European accent. And then he proceeded to inquire if this was Bob's apartment, using Bob's full name, even his middle initial. The wife was quite surprised to hear his inquiry and admitted that, yes, it was Bob's apartment all right. 'Ach, goot,' said the man. He said it with relief and enthusiasm, adding: 'Then ve have found him at last. Let me introduce ourselves, ve are your home teachers. May ve come in, please?' " The stake president gestured with his hand, held it high, signaling that a significant point was now to be made.

"And up to this time in her young life, Bob's wife had never heard the term *home teacher*, had never met a home teacher, did not know that home teaching was the basic communications function of Mormonism. She could not know, at that moment, what a monumental thing was happening at her humble threshold: that here in our great city, among millions of strangers, and several thousands of miles from her original home, diligent home teachers on assignment from a well-organized branch president were about to turn her young life completely around.

"She was not sensitive to this singular fact: that it was the priesthood of Almighty God standing at her entranceway asking to come in. But she did indeed invite them in, at which time the astonished husband jumped up, brushed aside the introductions, dropped his paper on the floor, and announced that he had to hurry out. And he did so, grabbing his coat and rushing down the hall, leaving the two home teachers and his wife standing a bit bewildered right there in the middle of the tiny living room."

The speaker took a long pause, staring down at the empty pulpit, though it was bare of notes. He looked up and continued.

"Bob returned to the apartment only after he was assured the two priesthood holders had gone by listening outside his door. His wife, however, was still quite animated with the pleasure she had received from their visit. He should have stayed, she told him. He would have enjoyed their visit, she said, learning the background of the two men, especially the older one, the dear old man from Austria. She would have continued on, telling more, except Bob stopped her, explaining that home teachers were part of the onerous system he thought they had escaped when they left the West. He informed her that this renewed contact with the LDS Church was distasteful to him and that he never wanted to see the home teachers again.

"But they did come again," the stake president continued. "They came back a few weeks later. This time Bob was legitimately out of the apartment, so his pleasant wife invited them in and thoroughly enjoyed their second visit, enjoyed it even more than the first. She went out of her way not to tell Bob about it or that she had surreptitiously agreed on still other visits in the months to come.

"It was the fourth month when the home teachers came—without Bob's foreknowledge—and caught him home. He was trapped in the kitchen, for he would not come out. So he stayed there and pretended not to hear or care what the home teachers taught his wife.

"They were now aware that she was not a member and that Bob had no desire to fellowship with them or the other

Saints in the little branch. But they kept coming faithfully, and each time they explained more of the gospel to Bob's interested wife. For she turned out to be one of the golden ones, the kind the missionaries knock on a thousand apartment doors trying to find. She believed every word they taught her, and she waited for their visits, wanting to hear more, to read more.

"By their eighth visit, Bob found himself listening very carefully from the kitchen. In fact, he made sure she told him when they were coming so he could be home. And by the ninth visit, he was also looking forward to the home teachers' arrival. It was on the tenth visit that he finally crept out and joined the other three in his living room. He even participated, answering questions about his employment, his background, his home and childhood in Utah. And as he relived those early years, the happy years of his childhood, those wonderful years with his family and friends—"

Suddenly the stake president's voice broke. He stood there at the pulpit unable to go on, wrestling silently for control of turbulent emotions. His listeners waited and wondered. Then he swallowed hard and spoke again.

"Yes," he said, quite overcome, "it was I."

Out came a snow-white handkerchief, and he dabbed at his eyes and waited.

"It was I who tried to run away from the Church and never tell my dear wife about the gospel and all she was missing. But the home teachers came, and they told her. Yes, and I was right there listening and learning and agreeing with them. A peculiar thing about Brother Gottlieb—some of you from the Third and Eighth Wards should remember him—Brother Gottlieb, our wonderful home teacher. He told us that in the German language his name literally means 'God-lover.' And he surely was. And he put into practice a powerful message from the Book of Mormon: that 'when ye are in the service of your fellow beings ye are only in the service of your God.' "[3]

He fumbled again at his face with his handkerchief.

"Well, wonderful old Brother Gottlieb was so kind and thoughtful of my wife and me that when he encouraged us to come meet the rest of the branch, all my resistance melted away. He took us into that old red brick building up on 83rd Street and introduced us to everyone as though we were his own family. We had never felt such warmth and friendship since arriving here.

"Looking back through the years, it is easy to see that I came to feel about Brother Gottlieb just as I had felt about my own father, buried back in Utah while I was in my youth."

Again the stake president held high a hand.

"And here is the point I wish to make in all of this," and he looked down at his wife, sitting surrounded by their children. "That Brother Gottlieb did something for my wife and me that all home teachers are capable of doing—but that all too many fail to do. And that is this: he was diligent in seeing us! He was faithful in continuously coming to teach us. He was enthusiastic in bringing his kind spirit right into our home. He did not teach us great sermons with mighty messages. He spoke softly about celestial things, about eternal marriage, about temples and prophets. And now and then he read to us meaningful passages from the scriptures and told us about the word of God, and that God loved us—and that he, Brother Gottlieb, loved us." Another hard swallow.

"He and the young boys who came with him never left without pronouncing a simple, heartfelt blessing on our tiny apartment and on us. We became convinced that he was sincerely interested in us. He fanned a spark of gospel concern in my heart, fanned it into flame, into a burning desire to win back what I had lost. He did this with his touching display of care and concern. He baptized my wife. He introduced us to everyone as his dear friends. He sat beside us in classes. He took us places in his car. He testified often of the truthfulness of the gospel—and we could not doubt him!"

The stake president carefully folded away his handkerchief and tucked it into his inside pocket.

"Brothers and sisters, when our leaders tell us that God himself has commanded priesthood holders to visit the homes of all members, to strengthen them and lift them up, and to encourage them to do their duty—well, I'm a believer. More than that, I stand before you all this day as a testimony to the fruits of home teaching. All that I am, all that I have and hold dear, I owe to this inspired program of the Lord.

"And I would pay this final tribute to dear old Brother Gottlieb, a lover of God, a lover of me and my family, by saying that he taught us the single most important thing in home teaching—"

The stake president raised both arms high above his head and solemnly said: "Brethren of the priesthood, the single most important thing in home teaching is simply *being there*—getting out of your house or apartment and getting into the homes of those families assigned for you to watch over. Sisters of Zion, for you it is in encouraging your husbands and sons to be constant in fulfilling their assigned stewardship. Nothing happens in home teaching until home teachers come into the home!"

Notes

1. D&C 121:44.
2. Priesthood Home Teaching Handbook (Salt Lake City: The Church of Jesus Christ of Latter-days Saints, 1967), p. 1.
3. Mosiah 2:17.

4

Achieving the Incredible Goal: 100-Percent Home Teaching

"I don't wish you to be offended at this question, Bishop, and let me remind you that we served together for three years on the high council before you were called as bishop, but are you really qualifying for that 100 percent in home teaching I see each month on your reports?"

The bishop stopped himself from laughing out loud. But he did display a big grin.

"Homer, my good brother, I *should* be offended. But you're not the first person in this stake to raise an eyebrow or throw a fiery dart of suspicion at those hard-won statistics we claim our brethren here are achieving every month."

"Well, then, answer my question," pressed the high councilor. He was slouched comfortably back in his chair. Both were seated in the bishop's office, having just completed a financial audit, having thanked and dismissed the ward clerk.

"Of course we're getting 100 percent, but we're also getting a little weary about all the kidding we have to take over it. So let me ask you a question." The bishop hunched forward, both elbows on his desk, his fingers laced together. "Why does a perfect home teaching record each month seem so incredible to everyone?"

"Why?" The high councilor lingered on the word, then squeezed his eyelids together into tight slits, his slate-blue eyes fixed firmly on the bishop. "Because 100 percent in anything is perfection, and perfection isn't obtainable in this life—or so we're told."

"Drivel," retorted the bishop. "You pay a full tithing. That's perfection right there. You're a 100-percent tithe payer."

"Yes, and I usually home teach all four of my families in a given month, as do many other brethren in this stake," the high councilor replied. "But you're saying that all of your home teachers are visiting all of their families every single month, month after month. Always. Always. It's the logistics of all those perfect numbers that boggle the mind, make it unbelievable. You're saying to the rest of the stake that your ward, collectively, is a perfect home teaching ward. And that's incredible."

The bishop delicately tapped his outstretched fingers in front of his open mouth, pretending a wide yawn. "No, seriously," said the high councilor. "To my knowledge, no ward in this stake—or maybe any stake—had ever claimed perfect home teaching for even one month. Your ward has reported perfection ever since you became the bishop." He glanced at the wall calendar. "Let's see, that's at least six months straight."

"And no one thinks it can be done? Has been done?" asked the amused bishop.

"No one thinks it can be done without jiggering the numbers somehow. That's why you have a lot of doubting Thomases among the other bishoprics, the other quorum presidencies. They can't do it. So how can you?"

The high councilor held up the stake quarterly report that had been lying on the desktop. "Back to my original question: are you really getting the 100-percent home teaching you're reporting, or do you have a special way of computing your records?"

The bishop crossed his legs and frowned. "I should be

offended at that question, Homer. But I'm not. What I really am is surprised that the other bishops and quorum presidencies are upset because of what we are accomplishing. They could accomplish it too—except for one big reason: they don't really try. If the truth were known, 100-percent home teaching really isn't that hard to get in a compact neighborhood like ours."

"So how do you get it?"

"All right, I'll tell you," said the bishop pleasantly. "I thought you'd never ask. But let's start at the beginning. You will remember that one of my assignments while I was on the high council was home teaching." He waited for a nod. "And one of the things I was doing was continually making presentations to bishoprics and quorum presidencies, trying to work up some enthusiasm for doing a better job of home teaching than our stake had been doing."

"So?"

"So when our ward was divided and I was called to be the bishop of a brand-new ward—after the initial shock had worn off—I found myself faced with the proposition of needing to organize the entire ward home teaching from the ground up." He paused, ruminating.

"And?"

"And so I did some very deep thinking, yes, and some considerable praying—praying about home teaching. Reading about home teaching. And there really hasn't been that much written about how to do it, certainly not in the scriptures. But Church leaders have always been preaching about it to us, telling us how vital it is. So I've become convinced. And since I had been running through the stake waving my arms and shouting, trying to convince the other wards they should increase their efforts, and since no dramatic increase ever happened because of my efforts, well, I decided I now had the perfect opportunity to prove to myself, or to anyone, that 100-percent home teaching was possible."

"I'm listening."

"And so I remembered a story my old stake president used to tell us when I lived back east, where the stake took in an entire city, where you didn't have three or four families to home teach, you had eight or ten, or even more! You couldn't step out of your home and start teaching across the street, the way we do here, but you had to drive miles and miles in a car—if you had one. The stake president was disappointed that we only had 66-percent home teaching for an entire year. We thought that was exceptional; he hated it. So he called the priesthood leaders together and told us about his three daughters—pretty teenage daughters.

"The stake president said that a few nights before, all three daughters had dates. Three boys came by, one at a time, and drove off with his three precious girls. He was lying in bed later that night wondering about them when he heard the first one come home. She stuck her head in the bedroom and reported that she was back and all was well. She went off to bed. Soon he heard the front door open again, and his second daughter came into the bedroom to report that she was back safe and sound. At that point, the stake president told us all, hammering on the pulpit as he said it—I remember his face getting red—that by *our* home teaching standards he could now turn out the light and go to sleep because he had 66 percent of his daughters safe and accounted for! He was very powerfully exercised. He really shook us up."

"And that story sparked you to set your new ward goals for 100-percent home teaching?" asked the waiting high councilor with a touch of skepticism.

"Not just the story, no," replied the bishop. "It was all a question of comparative attitudes."

"Say what?"

"Comparative attitudes," repeated the bishop. "Far away in that big city is a stake president beating on the pulpit and turning red because he is worried that only 66 percent of his people are being home taught, and here in our splendid suburb, just minutes from a temple, where almost half the people are LDS and transportation is no problem, it doesn't seem to matter to anybody that we're limping along with home teaching percentages below his. That's a don't-care attitude. It upset me.

"No one really listened when I came around as the high councilor trying to build home teaching fires under them. So I decided—as a new bishop in a new ward—that I would exercise a little concern and prove we could do better. I pledged myself to never miss a family on any given month. And I did it after reasoning that if everyone is important to the Lord then everyone should be important to me." After a few seconds he unclasped his hands, made a big fist of one of them, and dropped it with a thump on the desk.

"I got my new counselors to agree that we three would home teach the entire ward by ourselves that first month, though the ward wasn't even organized until the middle of the month."

"Now wait a minute," the surprised high councilor spoke up. "How could you possibly do that, just the three of you?"

Sunshine spread across the bishop's face as he continued. "We divided the ward into three sections. We took our three new ward clerks as companions. We simply dedicated the necessary nights to doing the job we'd prayerfully pledged ourselves to do."

"But you have—150 families?" asked the high councilor, not waiting for an answer. "That's fifty families you each had to teach."

"Yes, fifty families each, and only two weeks to home

teach them in." The bishop folded his arms on his chest and slowly said, "And it was easy—easy and fun."

"Fun?"

"We didn't even need two weeks. We did it, home taught the entire 150 families in less than a week. We did it by simply walking through the ward, going from door to door the first several nights. LDS families are so concentrated in our neighborhood—unlike in that big city—that we found many at home. People who weren't home we would phone the next day and make a firm appointment. We didn't stop and lounge around when we entered a home, and we didn't prattle about things that didn't matter. We introduced ourselves as the new bishopric. We inquired as to the well-being of the family—talked for a few meaningful minutes, mentioning that this was a home teaching visit and that we were doing the entire ward ourselves just to let all the people know this first month that we loved them. Then we asked if we might leave a blessing, and we left.

"We had nothing but success," the bishop said with energy. "We all knocked off at 9:30 each night and met, the three sets of us, at an ice-cream store, where we reported matters of note. One of the statements we kept hearing was from people who said they had rarely—in several cases never—been visited by home teachers."

"I cannot believe you could do that," the still-doubting high councilor exclaimed. "Fifty families in one week?"

"Well, ten a night for five nights; it was a grand start for us," the bishop responded. "It sent up a glorious signal to everyone, a signal that said everyone was important to the new bishopric. Can you imagine the kind of emphasis we put on home teaching to our priesthood brethren the next month when they got their families assigned? We made a big point of the fact that just three sets of home teachers visited the entire ward—fifty families each—and did not miss a single one." The bishop motioned behind him at the large organizational chart fixed to the wall.

"Sure, it took some scrambling and rearranging and a lot of phoning," he said. "But the important thing is—we did it. And it was like a big banner reading '100-PERCENT HOME TEACHING,' a banner we might have run up a flagpole—if we had had a flagpole. Everyone could see we had done it. From that month on, no pair of home teachers was willing to drop the ball, miss visiting their own families." His voice was confiding as he said, "Who would want to be the first failing home teachers after that?"

"But surely," protested the high councilor, "not everyone in the ward has your dedication for maintaining that pledge for perfection. Someone is bound to mess it up, miss a family—some busy elder, some careless high priest. Some family will slip out of town on vacation before being home taught. Eventually someone is bound to ruin your record." Another pause. "And maybe they already have. Just how can you be sure?"

The bishop was waiting for this question. "You're right. At the outset some indifferent brethren surfaced, brethren who don't care a bit about missing a family or two, months on end. Some are very lukewarm to the whole idea of home teaching. So we work with them. We attempt to convince them—lovingly, persuasively—that each family is important to us, not for the statistical report, not to 'gratify vain ambition,'[1] but because they are part of our ward family, and because we love them."

"But the logistics of this thing!" exclaimed the high councilor incredulously. "There are just too many people out there to keep track of, too many cracks for them to fall through.

"Yes, indeed," agreed the bishop. "And the worst problem is the priesthood holders who mislead us, saying they'll do it and don't, saying they did it—and didn't."

"But how can you keep track of all that?"

"It's become a polished plan now, and a strong one. It works. But in the beginning we were holding it together with bailing wire and Band-Aids."

"Oh, yes, a polished plan," the doubtful high councilor repeated. "This I've got to hear."

The bishop looked at him hard, staring for a long minute before continuing.

"Most wards don't tally up home teaching till the end of the month. Some wards only do it quarterly, that is, wait three months before asking the home teachers whom they've taught, whom they've missed."

"That's when the stake report is due," offered the high councilor. "That's why they wait three months."

"Exactly," replied the bishop. "And in our program, that just won't work. That means we don't know where we stand until it's too late to do anything about it. It means that we wouldn't know that a family has been missed until it's too late to go back in and make sure they do get home taught. So our closing date for home teaching is the twentieth of the month." He paused, pleased to note his listener's genuine attentiveness.

"If, for whatever reason, a family isn't visited by the twentieth of the month, then we take back the family and teach them ourselves, the quorum leaders or the bishopric. We call it 'original jurisdiction.' "

"Original what?" the high councilor howled, much galvanized by this term. "You can't do that. You can't send in substitute home teachers just because the proper home teachers didn't meet your arbitrary deadline."

"We can," said the bishop pleasantly, "and we do."

"No!" protested the high councilor. "That means that if your regular priesthood brethren drop the ball on a given month, you rush in the second string to save the day. Is that the thing to do? Does that let the family feel they're being loved, that they're important when they never know from one month to the next who their home teachers will be?"

"It's not the best way," said the bishop quietly. "But it's better than no home teachers at all. And it does send out several messages."

"What messages?"

"First, a message that the priesthood leaders and the bishopric do think each family is important. We're not going to let them go unvisited under any circumstances. And second, it tells them that their regular home teachers had a problem: too busy, out of town, forgot about them, or just simply failed to meet the ward's deadline." The bishop's eyes were fastened to his visitor. "And our experience has been that when we have applied original jurisdiction, the hit-or-miss home teachers quickly rededicate themselves, never letting it happen again."

"But is that really home teaching—having your minutemen rushing in after the twentieth of the month?" the high councilor persisted.

"We have established our priorities, Homer. First, we visit every home at least monthly. Second, we train the priesthood how to home teach properly. But the visits are more important than training the priesthood. That is, if an elder is unwilling to do his job, we will do it for him. If he continues to die on us, we'll rescind his calling as a home teacher." Then the bishop thoughtfully added, "But that hasn't happened yet."

"Oh, I don't know about this thing you're telling me," the high councilor wailed. "You're too willing to throw out a weak home teacher. Doesn't the gospel teach us to be longsuffering? to 'lift up the hands which hang down'?"[2]

"It does. But our first concern must be for the family, for fulfilling the Lord's commandment that worthy priesthood brethren visit in their home. If a home teacher can't do that, then it's somewhat like that difficult situation Nephi faced."

"Nephi? Nephi had problems with home teachers?" The high councilor could be droll when feeling cornered, but the bishop brushed his question aside.

"You'll recall that Nephi was commanded by the Spirit to cut off Laban's head one dark night in Jerusalem. Laban had refused to turn over Nephi's family records, though he'd already been paid an agreed price for them. But Nephi balked at killing Laban, now lying drunken and helpless at his feet. The Spirit insisted and thereby gives us a divine directive, saying: 'It is better that one man should perish than that a nation should dwindle and perish in unbelief.'[3] So in our ward, we think it is better that one disinclined home teacher should be released than that a family should dwindle and perish from his neglect."

"Well, maybe that makes sense," Homer said a bit grudgingly.

But the bishop pressed his point. "Let me give you an example of this. I was once in a ward where a well-meaning bishop attempted to activate a very wayward elder by calling him to teach the deacons quorum. As a consequence, ten or twelve deacons dwindled and nearly perished in unbelief before their unruly, uncaring, incapable adviser was released."

"Well, yes, but—"

"You know, Homer, you remind me of one of the young husbands in our ward. My counselor had just thanked the home teachers during priesthood meeting in the chapel for maintaining our 100-percent performance, as we had just finished the month. But when I came down off the stand, this young man stopped me and said, 'Bishop, we couldn't have had 100 percent because no one home taught us.' I reminded him that his home teachers couldn't find anyone at his apartment and so reported to me. I informed them that his wife was in the hospital, isolated, and that I could get in but they couldn't. So I instructed them that I would be his home teacher for that month. He heard me out and said, 'But you're not our home teacher; you're our bishop.' "

The bishop reached into a drawer and withdrew a pamphlet. "I had him step into this office and read him a paragraph from this little booklet. Here, let me read it to you: 'The family is the most important organization in time or eternity. The Church and all its organizations are service agencies to help families and individuals. Home teachers represent the Lord, the bishop, and the priesthood leader in making available to the family and the individual the help of the Church and all its organizations.'[4]

"I read him that very statement and explained that since his home teachers represent me, and when they could not find him at home—for he was with her almost every night—I simply took back my original jurisdiction."

The high councilor was softening. "So that's your program? When the home teachers can't do their visits, for whatever reason, then you fall back on the quorum leaders? you have them do it? Hmmm. And if they can't do it, then you, as the bishop, step in and qualify yourself."

"Neatly put, Homer. Yes, that's the way we've been getting a perfect record every month. It was awfully hard at first, putting a real workload on the high priest group leaders and the elders quorum presidency. But after a couple of months it evened out. The bishopric is almost never needed in the home teaching loop any more. It's the quorum leaders who have to keep things humming—lots of phone calls, lots of checking up. They're the ones running around trying to patch things up and locate missing persons. And you know what? I've never seen them happier with what they've accomplished. Successful home teaching is very rewarding, very meaningful."

"Well, yes, I—"

"We're really enthusiastic about this record we've got going. It's a team effort. The whole ward is involved. Now, when someone is going to be gone for the rest of the month and hasn't been home taught, they call their home teachers and hurry them up, or they even call me. They know they're important to us. They know they'll be missed; and no one wants to be the first family missed."

The bishop tilted back his chair, hands locked behind his head. "You see, Homer, it isn't the numbers we're interested in, although it may appear that way to outsiders. We want to minister instead of administer, just as the Savior did, one on one, touching individual lives. But to be able to minister, we have to learn to administer. We want to shepherd our flock instead of merely count sheep. But we have to know who they are—count the ninety and nine—before we can identify the one that's missing. We want to use home teaching, an inspired program that is often neglected or abused, to bless people, all the people in our ward family. And we know that God can't direct our footsteps until we move our feet. So it's up to us. We have to get out and hustle."

Homer had drunk in every word. He was touched by the bishop's honest concern about families. "And what about that doubting husband?" he asked. "Did he ever buy the fact that you could be his home teacher?"

The bishop laughed. "He was disappointed that he hadn't caught us—what was your word?—jiggering the home teaching report. He had to be reminded that I was with his wife and him in the hospital three evenings that month. And one time, I recalled, I even taught him how to administer to his wife with consecrated oil. So in a very real sense, I told him, I was not just a priesthood visitor, but I was also genuinely teaching him an important function of the priesthood."

The bishop picked up the pamphlet again and opened

it, saying: "But listen to this. There is still another statement in this home teaching booklet I wanted him to hear, reminding him how important his own calling was as a home teacher. Listen to what this latter-day apostle writes: " 'I adjudge this [home teaching] to be one of the greatest positions in the Church, a job of mammoth proportions. I think Paul put in perspective our positions in the Church when he said, identifying the true church, "God hath set some in the church, first apostles, secondarily prophets, thirdly teachers, after that miracles, then gifts of healings, helps . . . " (1 Corinthians 12:28). The Lord's perspective is that the true position of a teacher, of one who gets inspiration and does what these revelations appoint, places him in the number three position in the Church, just after those who guide and direct its destinies.' "[5] The high councilor sat in silence, pondering the weight of all he had been learning from the bishop. Deeply absorbed, he slowly nodded his agreement. When he finally stood to go, he was all smiles.

"Well, talk about teaching! That's powerful stuff you've been teaching me tonight. And the mystery is solved. I now know how you do it and why you work so hard to do it. It's a remarkable record you've established—yes, and a worthy one. I hope you always make your 100-percent goal." The bishop stood up and they shook hands warmly. "You would have been pleased with your elders quorum presidency last month," the high councilor said. "They handled themselves well on this very subject. I was sitting there in that room full of quorum presidencies, and just before the meeting started, some of them were kidding your leaders. They were claiming that in their wards they were concentrating on qualitative home teaching whereas your ward was merely concentrating on quantitative home teaching. This was obviously a classic case of sour grapes. Your president, Henry, came right back at them. He said: 'We believe you can't improve the quality unless you actually make the visit. And that's quantity.' " The high councilor took a step toward the door.

"Oops," the bishop blurted out, holding up a hand to stop his visitor from leaving. He lifted still another pamphlet from his open drawer, saying, "When our critics in the other wards try to position quality over quantity, my elders have been schooled to remember this great statement by President Ezra Taft Benson:

" 'Remember, both the quality and quantity of home teaching are essential in being an effective home teacher. You should have quality visits, but you should also make contact with each of your families each month. As shepherds to all of your families, both active and less active, you should not be content with only reaching the ninety and nine. Your goal should be 100 percent home teaching every month.' "[6]

The high councilor shook his head in agreement and patted the bishop affectionately on the back. "You've taught your brethren very well. You can be proud of them. They are obviously dedicated leaders of an unusually effective team, one with a marvelous drive toward perfection."

Then lowering his voice he added: "I wasn't going to admit this to you when I was challenging your records earlier, but you might as well hear it now, now that you've explained how serious home teaching is." He paused again, a little pain etching into his expression as he sighed and spoke. "My wife reminded me just the other day that we haven't had home teachers visit us since before last Christmas. She asks, 'Who have we offended to be so abandoned?' "

Notes

1. See D&C 121:37.
2. Hebrews 12:12.

3. 1 Nephi 4:13.
4. Bruce R. McConkie, *Let Every Man Learn His Duty* (Salt Lake City: The Church of Jesus Christ of Latter-day Saints), p. 2.
5. Ibid., p. 10.
6. *Conference Report,* April 1987, p. 63.

5

Home Teaching: An Outsider's Inside View

Brother Larrabee was always amused when he first entered a corporate manager's office. Furnishings were the focus of power. They conveyed the company image: traditional, leading-edge, or iconoclastic. Wood panels, hushed tones, leather chairs, and book-lined shelves—as an example—clearly signaled "traditional" to his trained eyes. The one thing he always found in a corporate manager's office was spaciousness, large windows with a commanding view, and elegant furnishings demonstrating a designer's expensive taste and flair.

However, this was his first time in a stake president's office, and he had been curious about how it would look. Now that he was sitting there he found himself surprised at its austerity: painfully small, no view, one large table, and a few chairs. The only special touches were two pictures on the wall: a recent photograph of the First Presidency and a large gold frame featuring an excellent color print, a famous painting of the Savior.

Brother Larrabee was a nationally recognized and widely read thinker and writer on modern organizations and the discipline of management. So on this first occasion in an administrative church office, he was warmly greeted and comfortably seated. If the stake president was guilty of gushing over his guest, it was excusable.

A few weeks back, having learned of Brother Larrabee's forthcoming baptism in his stake, the president had rushed to purchase the latest Larrabee book, a book for the decision-maker in the management of service institutions. The stake president had been able to identify with the many rewarding messages therein. The book had provoked him to rethink his own management of his business and of his stake. It opened his mind to wider horizons. It was after reading the book—and, especially, having been told of Brother Larrabee's sincere conversion—that the president had decided to ask him to speak in their forthcoming stake conference.

But today, being somewhat intimidated by the proximity of this famous author in his office, the president proffered the invitation to speak almost as soon as they were seated. Brother Larrabee admitted later to his wife that he was quite surprised with the abruptness of this challenge to address a Mormon audience, for he would certainly be out of his normal element—the familiar fields and faces of business managers. He was flattered to be asked. But Brother Larrabee was a meditative man. He did not rush to give a hasty answer. So the two sat facing each other for a few moments, each reflected in the burnished surface of the mahogany table. The new convert allowed his gaze to drift just beyond the waiting president, resting on the heavily framed picture of the Savior before he finally found himself agreeing to it.

Yes, he would be honored to speak in stake conference.

"You certainly won't have any trouble as a speaker," said the stake president earnestly after thanking him for accepting. "We all know of your tremendous success as a writer. You've obviously been in much demand as a speaker."

"I've spoken around," Brother Larrabee agreed with honest modesty. "However, you are not asking me to speak as an analyst of management orthodoxy but as what? the newest baptized member of the stake?"

"Well, yes, certainly. Everyone knows of your coming into the Church last week. We were all so pleased. And because of your prominence, well, there's going to be a lot of interest in the story of your conversion." The president did not want this business expert to feel his testimony was being exploited. After all, he was no stranger to Mormonism, so he added, "Because your children and wife have been active Latter-day Saints many years. Everyone knows that, too."

Brother Larrabee looked steadily at the president. "It is true my—what shall we call it, change of heart?—did not come fast. It is also true that I now have a burgeoning conviction this is Christ's church. I'll be pleased to speak on my newly settled belief."

"Well, hmmm, yes, that is what we would like to hear." The president was still a little embarrassed that he might seem to be rushing this conspicuous convert to the pulpit too swiftly, so to slacken any strain he was feeling, he threw in some small talk. "So tell me, Brother Larrabee, just what was the hardest thing you had to do to come into the Church?"

"The hardest thing I had to do was admit that for eighteen years my wife has been right."

The stake president's face creased into a bright smile. "Yes, I see. You've a nice sense of humor."

"No. I'm very serious," came the convert's calm reply. "I now accept the gospel as being thoroughly true. And while I am deeply in debt to my wife for eighteen years of perseverance, I still credit my immediate turnabout to the Mormon home teaching program—and to one home teacher in particular."

"Home teaching?"

Another glance at the Savior's portrait and Brother Larrabee continued. "Yes, I've experienced eighteen great years of growth, living happily with my wife, and eighteen years of silently observing a very revealing performance from a parade of widely vacillating home teachers."

"Come again?"

"I don't want to be unkind, President, but I believe I've run the gamut on types of home teachers. I've seen good home teachers, bad home teachers, and indifferent home teachers. And since we moved into your stake, well, I've been significantly influenced, seeking baptism, because of great home teachers."

"Hmmm, wait a moment. Bad home teachers?"

"Forgive me. I shouldn't say 'bad.' I suppose bad home teachers are those who never even bothered to knock on our door, for we have gone months and months with none at all. But in the many places we've lived, and over these many years, I have taken a keen interest in the LDS home teaching program. I am willing to say it is the sleeping giant of Mormonism. In fact, I've even used some of it in the management philosophy I've been responsible for. For me, home teaching is a special thing. I firmly believe it embraces what the academician would call 'afflatus theopneusty'—the divine influence."

Brother Larrabee's eyes never left his stake president's face. He was intense in what he said. "I heard every session of general conference last month, and I was especially uplifted to hear the president of the Church himself speak on home teaching, saying it was 'inspired from its inception—a program that touches hearts, changes lives, spiritually renews.'[1] And that's exactly what home teaching has done for me—and right here in your stake these past months."

"My goodness," the stake president responded. "Well, we're certainly pleased to hear that. And I'm impressed that you have been so attentive in your observations of home teaching."

"Yes, and I think I have finally caught the vision of

what the Lord has set up in terms of tractable control through managerial communications for the entire Church. And I marvel at the ingeniousness of the program, that home teaching will work in any setting—for the rich and the poor, in any climate, in any culture, in any economy. And while I wouldn't pretend to have done any serious research, yet I believe I've recently uncovered the capstone statement for home teaching. In business we would call this the 'vision' or the 'mission statement.' Interesting ecclesiastical terms," he said as an aside, "but now being used every day by progressive commercial organizations. I have even jotted that statement down. Here, let me read it to you."

And reaching into his inside coat pocket, Brother Larrabee drew out a small brown notebook from which he read: " 'Home teaching, properly functioning, brings to the house of each member two priesthood bearers divinely commissioned and authoritatively called into the service by their priesthood leader and bishop.' "[2]

"That's the most marvelous of mission statements for a communications resolve. It has cyclopean proportions," the convert stated, with some animation in his voice. "As a professional, dedicated as I am to organizational management, it is as strong a sign of the divinity of the Mormon Church as is the Book of Mormon!"

The stake president was surprised. "Why, I can't believe you are so caught up in home teaching that you actually carry around statements about it."

"Oh, my dear president, home teaching is one of the great treasures I've uncovered in my years of looking closely at your church."

"Our church," the president corrected.

"Our church," echoed the convert with a smile.

Now it was the president's turn to sit quietly and study the engaging face across the table. But only for a few moments, and then he stirred and spoke with a lowered voice, with confidentiality.

"Brother Larrabee, you have some special gifts, some special insights you obviously bring to Mormonism. You are the classic example of having been an accomplished outsider looking in. And before I ask you the question I'm anxious to ask, let me turn the tables on you and prove the value I place on your own wisdom." And as he spoke, the stake president reached out and picked up a large notebook lying on the table in front of him. Turning a few pages, he looked up and said with a note of triumph, "Ah, now, allow me to read something you wrote that I consider important enough to write down for my own use. Yes, and to share with my high council and bishops." And the president read: " 'Making resources productive is the specific job of management. Productivity of work is not the responsibility of the worker but the responsibility of management.' "

The stake president was delighted he could prove he had dug deeply into the Larrabee philosophy. "You see, that statement hit me very hard. You have said that if the productivity of my stake is to improve, then it must start with me."

The president closed the book but kept his finger between its pages. "I look at our stake statistics—our recorded productivity—and feel deeply the need to improve them. How can I get priesthood holders up and down the line to improve? How can I communicate the need for more support for the individual families? Well, your statement, simple though it seems, says that I should be making better use, more efficient use, of resources already available."

Brother Larrabee was pleasantly stirred. "Well now, president," he said, his eyes gleaming, "we have just come full cycle. The answer to your utilizing more of the unused resources of your stake lies in your own wonderful home teaching program. It's already in place. It just needs to be worked harder, used more properly—more consistently."

"Then let me ask you my burning question about home teaching," the president cut in, "because it represents a paradox that has puzzled me since long before I was called as president. Why will an active Latter-day Saint accept a mission call, sacrifice everything to travel to the other side of the world to fulfill it, knock on the doors of ten thousand strangers—and yet procrastinate simply traveling a few blocks or miles once a month to home teach his friends and neighbors, families of his faith?"

"Ah," the management analyst responded with gathering excitement. "That is a burning question. But there is no puzzle in it. Let me point out—in my humble opinion—the broad difference in the two callings. First, when a Mormon goes on a mission, it calls for a general celebration in the neighborhood: slaps on the back, a crowded farewell, laudatory speeches, his favorite hymns, and so on. He gets a grand sendoff at the airport with flags flying, bands playing, plenty of tears and hoopla. And even during his mission, he is continually reinforced with letters and packages of encouragement from home. It's hard for him to fail because of so many people in the system to prop him up, keeping him productive, keeping him going. He's almost guaranteed a repeat celebration at the airport when he completes his two years, and another crowded sacrament meeting for his homecoming. Plus," and Brother Larrabee held up his index finger, "he now wears a big medal on his chest, invisible though it may be, that says 'Honorably Returned Missionary.' "

The stake president sat, admiring this colorful convert's depth of understanding.

"But just measure the change of pace when that same excited, returned missionary receives the simple assignment of becoming a plain, everyday home teacher," the convert went on. "Missionaries are special; home teachers are everywhere. There may be a feeling that no fire-in-the-belly spirituality is needed for home teaching. For without proper understanding and vision, home teaching could seem humdrum to most priesthood holders. And there are no bands or shouts to send a home teacher off on his designated rounds every thirty days. His calling is now perfunctory, mechanical, ordinary, drab. He's expected to perform month after month, endlessly. There's no conclusion in sight, no let up, no special commendation, no celebration for a job well done."

The convert leaned forward, lowering his voice but charged with energy. "He's still going to be a home teacher when he dies, sometimes just stumbling along for years. Just a hit-or-miss, catch-as-catch-can home teacher." He sat back and sighed. "There's not a lot of glory in it. Glory is the stuff of missions."

The stake president was in painful agreement with what he was hearing. "But you've already qualified home teaching as being divinely inspired. Why can't the brethren be ignited, catch fire as home teachers—the same way you've just pointed out they feel when called as missionaries?"

"Ah, but my dear president, they can! And many of them do! It is true that home teaching is a lifetime task, and that over the years there may be an endless buildup of scar tissue. But dedicated and visionary home teachers also know that God isn't going to scrutinize them as much for degrees and diplomas as for scars. So to improve the home teaching in your stake, our brethren must catch the vision of what the Lord wants from his home teachers. And who is in charge of giving them that vision? Who makes the stake's 'resources productive and available to the stake's work force'?"

The stake president tapped the closed notebook still lying in his lap.

"Right!" thundered the convert. "It is the stake's appointed manager. It is you! And as I understand your chain of command, it is also your bishops, and then your quorum leaders." Brother Larrabee now rose to his feet. He always felt more comfortable standing or pacing as he talked.

"The best part about home teaching in your stake—our stake—is that it is working marvelously for some of us. I believe that home teaching is one of the most remarkable communication disciplines I've ever run across. Just imagine the scope of it! In the LDS membership, a church numbering in the millions, there is an inner corps of hundreds of thousands of men and boys—all volunteers, for no one is paid—who willingly take an assignment to visit that entire membership of millions at least once a month! That is astonishing in its scope. Where else in the world can you find such an amazing work force dedicated to doing so much good, and on such a continuous basis? Here, let me read you something I received in the mail today. You'll be amused at its timeliness."

Reaching into his inside coat pocket, Brother Larrabee retrieved his notebook and took from within its pages an envelope from which he withdrew several handwritten pages.

"This is a letter I just happened to receive today at my office. My wife hasn't even had a chance to read it yet. It is from our oldest daughter who is studying in Cambridge, England. Listen to her comments:

" 'It takes about half an hour to bike to our LDS church here, but it is well worth it. There are plenty of beautiful, huge chapels all over Cambridge where exquisite music is played. I have been to several Church of England services here, one of them in the most incredible cathedral. It is more stunning than Westminster and was begun in the year 1083. The music was glorious, but the service could not compare to the humble, strong spirit I feel in our little LDS meetinghouse. Those professional ministers conduct their worship service more for show. I don't think they care for the people gathered in their grand cathedral. They certainly don't check to see if anyone did his home teaching.' "

Brother Larrabee looked up. "While I appreciate the fact that my daughter has a splendid bias where religion is concerned, yet she is right about Episcopalian home teaching. It doesn't happen. It doesn't exist. No Church of England bishop has ever had the inspiration—or the interest—in setting up that spectacular network of people caring for people on a well-organized and consistent basis, laymen looking in, on assignment, over all the fellow members of their congregation. That is exclusively found in Mormonism. That's our home teaching with its amazing capability, producing astonishing results for families and individuals—and it surely turned me around these past months."

Brother Larrabee stopped his pacing and gazed again at the picture of the Savior. "But there is another side to home teaching, namely, that many of your priesthood holders fail to live up to its . . . " he cast about for the right words, "awesome potential. High potential is what you've got. What you want is high performance."

The stake president squirmed visibly. "I already know that much, unfortunately. But tell me more about why it works and why it doesn't. I would be genuinely interested in your analysis, your criticism."

"Criticism?" responded the convert quickly. "I didn't think that Mormon leadership took kindly to criticism." His smile returned as he said this, and he sank back into his chair, signaling a desire to continue the interview.

"You're right," said the president warmly. "But only criticism of Church doctrine. Any attempt to nullify or subvert the word of the Lord, the scriptures, or an inspired leader's counsel, is not tolerated. But a constructive critique of our own mortal efforts to fulfill divine counsel or to serve our membership—as we are striving to do with home teaching—yes, I want to hear that. That's constructive."

Then lifting the notebook in his lap back onto the table he added, "Criticism may not be agreeable sometimes, but it is necessary—and it can be helpful. I have heard it compared to the function of pain in the human body: it calls attention to an unhealthy state of things. And that can save lives. I suppose my own high council can be very critical of programs we are struggling to initiate or refine. But their criticism is given in a most helpful and uplifting manner. They're not pulling down. They're attempting to build up."

The president was amused to catch himself flailing out both arms to help demonstrate his high council's uplifting criticism. "But please, Brother Larrabee, do continue. Tell me how we can improve home teaching."

"I don't know what my observations are worth, limited as they are to my own home. But I will share my honest feelings with you," said the analyst, now relaxed in his chair. "But with this caution—that I don't pretend to be an expert in the Mormon mindset." He paused.

"However, I am an organizational observer, and I have silently monitored several dozen sets of home teachers who have come into my home over those eighteen years. Some did the job; some didn't. Some tried; some just didn't care." He halted this easy flow of words and then said, "We had one bright young man come to us when we lived on the coast who wanted to be a home teacher in the worst way—and that's how he did it."

"In the worst way?"

"Exactly."

The stake president's easy smile revealed his amusement, and the convert continued: "We lived in one ward where the bishopric decided that home teaching statistics would improve if all the home teachers met in the chapel—on a given night, men and boys together—where they would hear a rousing pep talk by their leaders on the dynamics of home teaching, and then everyone could rush out to complete all their monthly visits on that very same evening, ensuring that it all got done. They tried it and ended up laughing heartily over the futility of it all, because what they found, in fact, when they entered each home was that there were few complete families to hear their messages—only the sisters and children were there. The fathers and young men were out home teaching."

Twisting inwardly, the stake president remembered that as a new bishop, he had once toyed with the same idea.

"One of the most memorable home teaching visits I had occurred right after my wife joined the Church. That was before we had any children, and we had just purchased our first home, an old house with poor plumbing. My wife was gone and I was floundering to unplug the drain system when two gentlemen came to my door, strangers all dressed up in suits and ties, asking for my wife. I explained that she was gone. They explained that they were her home teachers. I don't believe I'd ever heard the term. Before I knew what was happening, however, they got it out of me that our drains were clogged and that I wasn't really smart enough to solve that situation. It became evident, as we three discussed the problem, that they had solutions—and were more than willing to share them with me.

"When my wife walked up our street, she was astonished to discover a man in a business suit crouching on top of our roof poking our garden hose down a pipe. She hurried inside and found still another well-dressed gentleman perched on the edge of her bathtub stuffing a towel into the sink; and as she stood there bewildered, she could hear my muffled voice coming from beneath the bathroom floor shouting, 'Shall I turn it on? Can you hear me?' "

Brother Larrabee's eyes wrinkled in merriment at the memory of this scene. Then he said reflectively, "Looking back now, President, I do believe those two first brothers possibly summed up the entire essence of home teaching. They had come unbidden to my door, uncovered a problem that obviously overwhelmed me, recognized I needed help—and then neither of them hesitated climbing onto my roof and splashing water on their suits in finally solving my difficulties. And though I can't remember their names now, and that was the first time I had ever met them, yet I would have to label them great exemplars of Mormon home teaching." He paused and added, "They were a class act."

"Hmmm, a class act indeed." The president once again studied the face of his guest, then asked, "Tell me, Brother Larrabee, I hear that term again and again. What does it mean to you, a class act?"

The merry eyes smoothed out, narrowed, penetrated. "I was reading the other day about William McKinley campaigning for reelection as president of the United States in 1900. He was standing at the back of the train as it slowly pulled away from the crowd that had just listened to his campaign speech. He had taken off his leather gloves while speaking and then to wave, and now that the crowd was nearly out of sight he pulled them on to warm his cold hands. Expensive pigskin gloves, they were. But he fumbled one, and it fell over the railing and off the back of the train right onto the track. He immediately pulled off the other glove and threw it out, and it landed beside its mate. The several men standing with him were astonished at this sudden act until he explained, 'There is nothing more maddening or more disappointing than finding just one glove.'

"I thought to myself when I read that, now that is a class act—totally unselfish, thoughtful of others, and done in an instant. No mulling over the thing, arguing mentally what was best to do. And you see, President, that is what I got from those two well-dressed home teachers the day my drain was clogged. They never hesitated once they saw the problem. They were totally committed to doing the best thing to help me—no strings attached. Yes, I'll put them right there alongside President McKinley. They were a class act."

"What other home teachers stand out in your mind?" the president asked.

"When we lived in Washington, D.C., we had a difficult one. He rarely missed seeing us monthly, but when he came, always alone, he would dominate any effort at family dialogue. He loved to quote scriptures, so his visits were more like a one-man scriptural treatise, a sermon. This somewhat embarrassed my wife, for I was especially not interested in looking at Mormonism then, and he was determined to convert me through his eloquent and liberal quotations from the Bible and Book of Mormon. He had an additional fetish, however. He never called ahead for an appointment. He liked to surprise us. So often I would not be home when he just dropped in, and my wife would admit later that without me he turned the full fire of his sermonizing on our little children.

"My wife tried to insulate me from him. For you must understand that she suffered a fundamental ambivalence when he was around. Two truly conflicting emotions: she wanted very much for me to become interested in the Church, but she didn't want me exposed to the only representative of the Church coming into our home, this oppressive and bombastic home teacher. And my dear wife—she would never think of asking a bishop to reassign our home teacher—finally agreed that one of her worst moments came the night he dropped in and found her dragging around under the weather and struggling with two sick children, one of them a babe in arms who continually cried. The house was in a mess, and she had left two older children unattended in the bathtub to answer the door. And there she found her home teacher ready to stride in, once again without an appointment.

"So he plunked himself right down on the couch and launched into his scriptural presentation regardless of the water fight or shrieks going on in the bathroom, or the two wailing children in her lap. It was a masterpiece of insensitivity. He wasn't concerned with her needs. He had prepared a scriptural message. He enjoyed ventilating his ideas, and he was determined to give them, come what may."

Brother Larrabee rubbed his hands thoughtfully.

"She was in tears when I finally got home. After I calmed her down, I asked her what his message had been. She said she didn't know because she couldn't hear it for the clamor of the children squirming in her lap."

Both men frowned sympathetically at each other. But the president was quick to break the silence. "So you've had some interesting times with home teachers over the years, and you've said you had some that cared and some that didn't. Tell me, would you feel it's easy—early on—to discern strong home teachers from weak ones?"

Brother Larrabee was amused. "Strong versus weak? Let's call them effective versus ineffective, because that's the way we have to evaluate workers in the business world. They are all measured against the *effectiveness* of their performance." He said these last words slowly, with emphasis. "And they are paid accordingly, rewarded, given proper bonuses as dictated by the profitability they produce." He paused. "And the other side of the coin—ineffectiveness—is very serious. If they prove to be nonproducers, then we have only three alternatives: one, we can retrain them; two, we can transfer them to something less demanding, less rewarding; or three, we can simply take them off the payroll and eliminate their salaries from bloating our overhead. We terminate them. And that's unpleasant. But then, my Mormon children have always sung a song about 'the world has no use for the drone.' "

The two men sat silent for a long moment.

"And the business world agrees with that sentiment," the president said with finality.

"Because all service in the Mormon Church is voluntary," Brother Larrabee went on, "you can't just fire people. You've got to be grateful for whatever service they freely give. But in the case of home teachers, why should Mormon managers tolerate a slothful, unproductive effort any more than concerned business executives do? Home teaching is too vital, too valuable a function when it's properly done." That last comment was added with a steely-eyed smile.

The president was pricked by another twinge of conscience from this management analyst's high opinion of a Church program he'd always dismissed as being rather routine. "It's obvious you have certainly experienced a broad spectrum of effectiveness with your home teachers," he said. "But answer my original question: how early can you as a discerning father measure effective versus ineffective teachers new in your home?"

"It's almost immediate. Almost as soon as they walk through the door, come into the house. Some basic home teaching mistakes will inevitably tip the family off that we have got ourselves another pair of heedless, nonchalant, unmotivated teachers."

"Inevitably? Explain that, please."

"Inevitability," repeated Brother Larrabee, "is like that story they tell about a National League umpire we used to watch when we went to baseball games in New York. After an overzealous rookie threw his bat high into the air to protest a called strike, the umpire said, 'Son, if that bat comes down, you're out of this game.' " He chuckled to himself.

"So when I took the measure of the *ineffective* performance of a new set of home teachers, I could tell they were not going to have the skills or concern to help my family. And they certainly wouldn't be able to persuade me to get closer to the gospel—which my wife and children wanted. They had flung the bat in the air. It was inevitable that they were out of the game, the game they were playing so ineptly in my own living room."

"An excellent analogy," the president commented, tapped his fingers on his notebook as he reflected and then said: "But on balance you say you've had good home teachers too?"

"Oh, President, not good ones—great ones! A few years back—and at that time I was a chain smoker, had smoked long before my wife joined the Church—we had a home teacher that really concentrated on me, on things I was interested in. When he discovered I took an inordinate delight in trout fishing, he invited me to join him and several of his LDS friends on an overnight hike up to a remote mountain lake. I agreed to go and got quite excited about the trip. I felt I was in as good a shape physically as were he and his two friends when we started out, but by the time we reached the top of the ridge, and with the fifty-pound pack I was carrying, why, I was astonishingly out of breath. We stood there, the four of us, drinking in the scene below, standing high on the cliff overlooking our lake. And all we could hear in the silence of that glorious setting was my labored breathing.

"It became so obvious that I couldn't catch my breath, and that their lungs were in great shape, that I acknowledged my weakness by taking out the four packages of cigarettes from my pack and throwing them as far out over that beautiful valley as I could. It was a mortifying moment of total acquiescence for me."

"But a great teaching moment regarding the Word of Wisdom?" the stake president inquired.

"No, my great teaching moment caught up with me the next day when I found myself spending all morning stumbling through the rocks and brush at the foot of the cliff—searching hopelessly for my cigarettes." The analyst studied the fingers that for so many years had held his cigarettes. "And I haven't smoked since that very revealing trip with my home teacher."

He looked back up at the president and said, "But the home teacher we've enjoyed these past months since coming into your stake, he is one of the finest men I have ever met—in or out of the Church. I couldn't be too effusive in my praise of him. He approaches the ideal prototype as a home teacher."

"That's high praise."

"High praise, but merited," the convert replied. "I know a dozen companies that would pay a high price to get a man of Bob Crabtree's sensitivities on their management team."

"Bob Crabtree, the elders quorum president?"

"He's my home teacher, yes," replied Brother Larrabee with a little ring of pride in his voice. "It was he who personally led me down those white tile steps and into the waters of baptism last week. And let me compliment our ward leaders on assigning him to our family, to me. I have since learned that the Church program now is to send the strongest home teachers to the most needful homes. Assigning Bob Crabtree to me was right on target. For if anyone in the ward needed a great home teacher, I did. And you talk about my sensing the inevitable, why, I knew the minute he crossed our threshold that he was going to have the spirituality to finally answer my most difficult questions, bring me all the way into the Church." Brother Larrabee leaned forward. "You should have Bob Crabtree write the how-to manual on becoming a winning home teacher. He has the vision; he knows how to articulate the Lord's program."

The president's interest continued to climb. "So tell me, Brother Larrabee, what immediate signs did you recognize when Brother Crabtree came into your home, those positive signs that told you he was going to be effective?"

"He did everything right. He did his homework. He knew all about us—about me. He counseled with our previous home teachers. He talked privately with my wife. He knew the children already, and they really were attracted to him. He told me he was going to be our home teacher before I actually met him. Then he called for an appointment on the phone and was so pleasant in that quick conversation that he had my interest up. And when he came into our house, well, you could actually feel his genuine concern for us. He didn't barge in like so many. He was quiet, respectful, careful in introducing the young man with him, unobtrusive in introducing himself. And best of all, he didn't wait until the end of the month to make his visit. In fact, as he built a strong relationship with me, he came more often than your mandated thirty days. You see, he was sincerely interested in us.

"He made a strong point in explaining that though he knew I was not a member of the church he represented, and that his religious affiliation was only with my wife and children, yet he and his young companion regarded me as the head of the home. He said they would always defer to me, abide by my wishes. Then he asked if they might hear from me. Would I give them direction in what they should present to my family? That's the best any home teacher had ever made me feel."

"And you requested a religious message each time?" asked the president.

"Well, that's where I came to enjoy Bob Crabtree so much. We always chatted about a specific subject for our next visit. It wasn't always a doctrinal subject; but it always involved achieving a happier life. And I came to discover that's really the essence of the gospel anyway.

"When they returned, they both came thoroughly prepared. The meat of their message wasn't aimed at me only but very much involved my whole family. And they always asked questions, getting participation from all of us and letting my children feel that their opinions were important. Brother Crabtree even made assignments to us, getting everyone in the family united, which made it very pleasant for each of us to contribute during the next visit—as we had been assigned. And he cheered us on lustily, was high in his praise of us."

The convert's face was aglow in praise of his home teacher. "He was most considerate and helpful; didn't embarrass any of us. And he didn't lean on me—as so many have in the past—trying to provoke me into being baptized, trying to prove I was making a big mistake in not being LDS. And best of all, he was punctual and pleasant, and he always left us wanting to hear more. Those qualities are rare in your everyday home teachers. They are rare in the business world."

"Hmmm," murmured the president reflectively. "And so just what kinds of things did he teach you?"

"We had quite an interesting little review, that very first meeting, of what would be helpful to me, to my wife and children. We suggested some goals to each other, the home teachers and the family together, talked about where those various subjects would lead us. Then each visit with Brother Crabtree and his young companions—for they were changed around—progressively kept my family and me on track accomplishing those goals. It was a remarkable unfolding of vital information about life and its purposes, death and its meaning, family relations and how to improve them. I came to discover these were all essential gospel subjects.

"I became quite intrigued about what we were being

taught, what I was learning, and I had to start reading the books that were being quoted in our meetings just to keep up with my children. It was an amazing period of growth for me. It was a wonder for my wife to see me finally taking hold."

Brother Larrabee tugged at his ear, remembering the pleasure of those experiences. "And there were plenty of occasions when I threw their train off the track—my family and the home teachers—with questions coming off the wall, playing the devil's advocate. But they were very patient with me, and Brother Crabtree was very wise in acting as facilitator, fielding my questions and pulling many doctrinal answers for me from my own wife and children."

In his enthusiasm, the convert had worked his way forward, perching on the edge of his chair. The president thought he might spring up at any moment.

"You see, he knew I would be surprised, even astonished—yes, and pleased—to see this demonstration right within my own home: that Sunday School lessons had deeply qualified my children, even the younger ones, to understand life and its significant values, better—oh, so much, much better than their father." He clapped his hand on his knee. "And there was always time, before and after what was obviously the meat of these instructive visits, for miscellaneous talk, where Brother Crabtree always managed to pull whatever subject I happened to bring up right back into gospel focus."

"Explain that."

"Well, no matter what I would say, no matter how extraneous or far afield from gospel subjects I would wander in feeding my own interests, he would artfully refocus my subjects back to something pertaining to a teaching message on the Church. If I started talking baseball, he would casually mention that the great Dale Murphy or Harmon Killibrew were LDS. If it was golf, he could name the current

Latter-day Saints on the pro tour. If I talked fishing, he reminded me that the Apostle Peter was a fisherman. If I mentioned politics, he soon had us discussing the fact that Ezra Taft Benson was once the United States Secretary of Agriculture—and the only original cabinet member to stay with the president for all eight years of the Eisenhower administration."

Brother Larrabee folded his arms with finality over his chest. "Yes, he kept me on a straight and productive course. And he did it with good taste and humor, and with touching spirituality." Another long pause, and then his voice caught as he went on. "He was the first man who ever helped me find the courage to pray before my family. It was something we worked on privately. And when I finally knelt and prayed that first time, why, he was kneeling right beside me." A painful pause. "And with everyone's eyes shut, Bob slipped an arm around my shoulders."

The convert was charged with strong emotion. But he concluded with a shining smile.

"My home teacher, Brother Crabtree, has become a wonderful friend—and a marvelous advocate for Christ. I would have to say that it was his spirituality, his pure love of God, his continually expressing his testimony as to the validity of all the Church stands for—it was the weight of all of it that persuaded me to start my own personal prayers, my concerned study of the scriptures, and finally my request to be baptized."

He was finished. The convert had given rich and convincing testimony to the attentive stake president of his solid conversion to the gospel of Jesus Christ. He would make a touching contribution at the forthcoming stake conference, the president thought to himself. Yes, there was inspiration in asking him to speak. No doubt about that.

They fell silent one final time, looking affably at one

another. Then the president spoke: "This has been a most enlightening interview for me, good brother. I feel very close to you because of it. I will look forward with great interest to your conference address."

The convert smiled, nodded his accord.

"But I would like to point out that you have done something very special for me in this brief conversation, Brother Larrabee. You have awakened some things within me regarding home teaching. A sleeping giant, you called it. As powerful a proof that our church is true as is the Book of Mormon, you said."

The convert smiled steadily; his gaze never wavered.

"High potential is what we have, but high performance is what we need. You said that also." The president looked around the empty room. "And so you have stirred up some strong creative juices within me." He turned his head back, carefully considering the convert reflected in the polished table. "You've caused some ideas to foment, which, I suppose, is why you have earned the reputation you have."

The convert's eyes stayed fastened to the president's face.

"So I am making an additional request of you. This discussion of ours has provoked me to feel there is much more I can do personally in managing the home teaching in this stake. We've already agreed, you and I, that I am in charge of training priesthood leaders, and, well, I suspect I may have been somewhat derelict—in regards to home teaching. I want to call a special meeting of some key stake people and set up a panel to review some of the ways we could improve ourselves in that sacred assignment." The president was an energetic and decisive man, but now he paused dramatically.

"And I would like you to be a resource member of that discussion group." The president opened his notebook and turned to a calendar. "You say your home teacher should write the how-to book on home teaching. No, dear brother. It is you who have seen the good, the bad, the indifferent. Best of all, it is you who have the professional skills to make a transcending contribution to the rest of us. You see our program with the freshness of outside eyes. We want your point of view."

The convert moved to speak, but the president pressed on. "I would like you to make a presentation to our discussion group where you profile the effective home teacher, where you outline his attributes, his attitudes, his skills. I know you can do this. And the Lord will inspire you in the doing. This will be your first calling as a Latter-day Saint, to make your special contribution in helping us define and understand home teaching effectiveness."

As the president leaned forward, reaching his right hand across the wide table, he said, "I believe some of the home teachers in this stake would improve themselves if they could catch the marvelous spirit and vision of inspired home teaching. Will you help me in this task? Help us to bring others closer to Christ as you have just experienced—through inspired home teaching?"

Notes

1. Ezra Taft Benson, *Conference Report*, April 1987.
2. Marion G. Romney, *Conference Report*, April 1966.

6

Seeking the Spirit

The multipurpose room in the stake center could seat seventy or eighty people comfortably. On this occasion, however, the priesthood leadership turnout to hear the results of the stake president's study on home teaching had created an unaccustomed crush. Some of this heightened interest had been stirred up by the rumor that Brother Larrabee, "one of the foremost philosophers of American business management," was going to present a critical analysis—an "outsider's" critiquc—of home teaching.

Measuring the heavy turnout with his eye, the stake executive secretary suggested they remove themselves into the cultural hall and set up chairs there. But, no, the president desired the intimate control of this smaller room. Additional chairs were quickly crowded in and everyone was finally seated. Following the hymn and prayer, the stake president was on his feet greeting, introducing, conducting.

"Brethren, we have an unusual opportunity tonight. A little later on, you are going to be given a printed outline, a booklet profiling the prototype of what this task group considers to be a Christlike home teacher—not an easy enterprise for this little group on the front row. But let me point out that this committee includes a bishop who has led his ward in achieving 100-percent home teaching since it was organized, two erstwhile mission presidents, a former regional representative of the Council of the Twelve, and three hard-working elders quorum presidents, as well as two senior high councilors and, of course, your stake presidency—all home teachers with vast years of experience on the front lines.

"Another key member of our committee is Brother Larrabee, whom we all enjoyed hearing last stake conference. His was a singular contribution, not because he has been an effective home teacher or even a longtime home teacher but, more important perhaps, because his recent conversion was precipitated by effective home teaching. His value to our task group was his newness, his freshness. He is so very new in the Church that he still represents an outsider looking in. Oftentimes we get a different perspective when we see ourselves through other people's eyes. And that was most helpful."

The president said this because he was keenly aware that rumors had run rife about Brother Larrabee. It had been suggested by some that because he was not "churchbroke" he had played the devil's advocate when orthodox discussions were probing the depths of home teaching techniques. Whispers also had it that his corporate management expertise made him a standout maverick on the committee. Mutterings and murmurings had been spent speculating over his value, asking what genuine contribution such a lifetime gentile might make to a disciplined committee of fourth-generation Mormons reviewing a function as fundamental as home teaching.

"In this regard," the president was saying, "allow me now to share with you part of an essay I first read some years ago: 'I don't care whether it's a business association, a labor union, a political party, or a church—all are guilty of the sin of talking to themselves. Democrats attend Democratic meetings, Republicans turn out for Republican rallies, union members go to their meetings, and the business people attend theirs. They all usually invite, and applaud, speakers they already agree with, and the speakers feel gratified because they evoke hearty applause. But nobody has had his opinions challenged, nor his beliefs questioned.' "[1]

The president looked up from the paper in his hand. "So our first presenter tonight is Brother Larrabee, a priest in the Ninth Ward, and doubtless the least experienced home teacher among us. I have asked him to share his feelings about home teaching—especially after the many meetings and discussions he has sat through since being called as a resource person to this committee. He will also introduce a written declaration to which we have all contributed. We feel it will be very helpful as you strengthen the individuals and families within your assigned stewardships. It is titled simply, "Guidelines for Home Teachers." And Brother Larrabee will also review some foundation qualities we all feel to be necessary for an achieving home teacher."

Even as he stood to address the group, Brother Larrabee noted there was not a smile in fifteen rows of faces. "Gentlemen—ahem, brethren—and I'll just have to get used to this new terminology. Please be patient with me." He noted a rash of faint smiles break out. "I greatly appreciate the opportunity our stake president has given in allowing me to lead off this evening. I see that some of you have notebooks. Excellent. The shortest pencil is more permanent than the longest memory." He was a born teacher and could never resist scattering about his homilies. "But the major thrust of our presentation is already printed and will be passed out later." He gestured toward a pile of booklets stacked on the table behind him.

"Let me explain what a refreshing change of pace it has been for me to work with this committee, this task group, a group that always prayed in Christ's name before and after every meeting, petitioning our Father in heaven for success. That was an astonishing anomaly for me. I was also vitally interested in observing our stake president in action—leading discussions, defining our mission, assigning the gathering and sifting and collating of selected materials. Let me say very simply that I have come through this experience convinced that God indeed inspires our president. Under his enlivened direction we have researched and drawn from a wealth of powerful statements already made on the subject of the home teaching program."

Brother Larrabee looked about—a commanding figure, though he was not tall—making sure he had eye contact with each attentive row of faces.

"You have just heard in our president's introduction of me that I participated in our attempt to profile the perfect home teacher. That is too ambitious a task for mere mortals, and especially for me, an obvious outsider. But I am naive enough that I truly tried to help. There were many times when I apologized to my associates on the committee for my great lack of knowledge, for my perpetual challenging of what was being done and why. I suspect it made some of them feel they were being put on the defensive. Therefore, I must acknowledge that I hold out great respect for each of them, and for you—all of you—priesthood leaders. You may not know what strength you hold as a body of dedicated men."

His humility and appreciation were genuine, and the sea of bland faces was warming up. He continued: "Since I am quick to admit that you already know much more about our subject than do I, please bear with me. Most of what I shall say now is from me, my observations of qualities I have discovered and identified for myself in sifting through so much that has been written and said regarding home teaching. I am sharing with you, therefore, a neophyte's fragile and superficial observations." He reached behind him, picking up a booklet from the table. "But the materials collected in here under the direction of our stake presidency, well, they are solid gold.

"So to commence my own presentation, allow me, please, to involve you with an illustration, a revealing little story that I believe has everything to do with our discussion tonight. It is the story of a young married man whose company required him to spend a few weeks in New York City to receive some training at the corporate offices. Because of the length of his stay, he was allowed to bring his wife and little boy with him, and it was arranged that they would stay in one of the company's apartments on 5th Avenue, overlooking Central Park. It became a routine for the young man, after spending a hard day in training, to take the little boy for a walk in Central Park. So every day the father and son would stroll through this pleasant park, and every day they would end their walk in front of the famous bronze statue of General William Tecumseh Sherman, towering fifteen feet in the air, a heroic figure in full military regalia sitting astride a great horse and with his sword upraised, symbolically pointing skyward.

"On their first confrontation with General Sherman's grandiose statue, the father—the weather being chilly—took off his hat in mock salute and said, 'Hello, Sherman.' The little boy took off his own small cap in the same manner and mimicked his father, 'Hello, Sherman.'

"This practice continued every working day during their weeks in the city until that sad day when they took their final stroll before their departure for home. So this walk was especially touching, even a bit nostalgic. They had thoroughly enjoyed their wanderings through the park together.

"This time when they ended up at Sherman's statue, the father altered his routine. Instead of saluting by holding high his hat, he now placed it over his heart and sorrowfully said, 'Good-bye, Sherman.' The little boy followed suit: 'Good-bye, Sherman.'

"And after this touching little ritual, while they both held their pose before this dynamic military leader, the little boy spoke up again, asking, 'Daddy, who is that man sitting on Sherman?' "

Surprised laughter erupted in the crowded room.

Brother Larrabee waited till it faded and then said, "Brethren, tonight we are talking about the difference between perception and reality!" He lifted a hand into the air. "Tonight we are going to see if you view your home teaching assignments as a mere monthly function, a social call, a quasi-spiritual quick fix—with a little teaching here and a scripture thrown in there, mingled with comments on the weather or the social scene in the ward. Or whether you see home teaching for what it really is, one of the most powerful communications tools ever devised by our loving Father—and commanded by him of honorable men, men such as yourselves, men especially called to serve the spiritual and temporal needs of families and individuals in God's kingdom on earth.

"With what eyes do you view the home teaching assignment you've been given? Are you like the wise and mature father standing before Sherman's statue, seeing—recognizing—with awe and respect one of the greatest military strategists in the history of American warfare?" He seemed to tower over them, waiting to pounce on anyone who would dare attempt an answer. "Or are you like the ingenuous, candid little boy, who sees only a horse?"

Fifteen rows of eyes were riveted to him.

"How do you minister to the families you've been assigned? Are you concentrating the God-given powers of your priesthood, stirring up the abundance of charity in your heart for them, praying and preparing anxiously for your visits to be effective and motivating? Are you concerned? solicitous? troubled? uneasy? watchful? cautious? vigilant? circumspect? Are you striving continually to identify and support their needs? Or are you seeing only the horse? Saying with a little boy's childish view of things that there's really no need to look deeply at this family. No troubles here. No need for concern. All's well, yea, verily, all's well in Zion. In fact, some may say, if we didn't even look in on them this month, why, it wouldn't really matter. All's well!"

He was a new convert, but he knew his Book of Mormon.

"Gentlemen, I'm not here to reproach anyone. I'm here to tell you how overwhelmed I have become with the greatness of the Mormon organization. I believe it to be inspired. I joined this Church because of that conviction. Home teaching can bond the Saints together and bring the spirit of the gospel into every home and family, regardless of their measure of faith, their love of God, or even their attendance in Sabbath meetings.

"It is a fact that my family had home teachers assigned eighteen years ago, immediately after my wife's baptism. Therefore I have had this singular advantage—that for eighteen years I have been looking directly at Mormonism. My view, my focus of the Church—because I never attended any meetings—came by looking through the only window that was opened to me—our home teachers."

He was beginning to pace before the group now.

"In all candor I must confess to you that sometimes the window was too dark to see much, while at other times it was crystal clear. Yet, during some periods, it was entirely shut, for no one came to us. My vision, my view of God's true church, all depended on the caliber and capacity of my home teachers. If the quality of home teachers was indispensable to my seeing the light of the gospel, I suggest it could be just as paramount to others, to stumbling, searching souls you and your quorums are called and assigned to home teach right now.

"I learned long ago from a pair of excellent home teachers that Joseph Smith was once asked by a journalist what the difference was between Mormonism and all of the other churches. This question begged for a very involved answer because there is a labyrinthian wealth of differences, vast disparities, between Mormonism and any other religion. But Joseph Smith—wise man that he was—stated all of those difference in one simple sentence: 'We have the Holy Ghost.' "

Brother Larrabee stopped pacing. "Let me ask you a reflective, rhetorical question: Do your own home teachers bring the Holy Ghost with them when they enter your home? Can you feel it? When you and your companion home teach, do you ever agonize in your own spiritual preparation before going into the homes of others? Do you plead that the Holy Ghost will be companion to you in all that you do and say? Have you been moved by that Spirit to praise your families' good works? Have you been spiritually moved to love them? spiritually motivated to encourage them? to chide them? to challenge them? to call them to repentance?"

He moved again, several steps to the center, until he was directly in front of the stake president.

"President, I was not LDS when my wife encouraged me to take her through the visitors' center at Liberty Jail one summer when we were driving through Missouri. But I was most interested in inspecting firsthand that restructured dungeon with its original stone floor where Joseph Smith had been chained in 1838. I saw those very stones upon which he was forced to sleep for six bitter winter months. Then I looked up and read the astonishing revelation God had given him while he was so cruelly shackled to those stones. It is a sublime and heavenly message, now artfully, carefully carved in the great marble wall that surrounds that little jail."

He had spoken directly to the president in a loud voice for all to hear, but now he looked up, his narrowed eyes sweeping the entire group. "When I considered Joseph's miserable circumstances—illegally held by his enemies while his Latter-day Saints were being scattered and driven across snowbound Missouri, forced to abandon farms and homes by the governor's wretched order to exterminate them—I wondered how a prophet would comment on such a seeming defeat. What would a true prophet be inspired to write in the midst of such monumental misery?

"And I reminded myself that this was the same prophet who had already offended many by announcing that only his church had the gift of the Holy Ghost." Brother Larrabee now picked up one of the booklets again, holding it high, then brought it down to his eye level and opened it.

"Let me read you what he wrote from our booklet 'Guidelines for Home Teachers.' And let me say that I had entirely forgotten it until members of the committee brought it forth and made it the center of our major discussion." The convert seemed to draw himself up, standing straighter, taller than before. "These words were spiritually whispered to an imprisoned, impoverished prophet. However, I agree with our president: they should be transcendent in the minds of home teachers everywhere whenever we plan our visits, whenever we are in the homes assigned to us—and whenever we are in our own homes. This is God's counsel on how priesthood holders should use priesthood authority. These instructions—in my judgment, and as a newcomer to the Church, yes, but one with some considerable experience in assessing organizations—these instructions, I repeat, are the consummate guide for home teachers who would honorably fulfill their assignments."

Having said all of this, Brother Larrabee now read with

a clear, ringing voice, the following: 'No power or influence can or ought to be maintained by virtue of the priesthood, only by persuasion, by long-suffering, by gentleness and meekness, and by love unfeigned; by kindness, and pure knowledge, which shall greatly enlarge the soul without hypocrisy, and without guile—reproving betimes with sharpness, when moved upon by the Holy Ghost; and then showing forth afterwards an increase of love toward him whom thou hast reproved, lest he esteem thee to be his enemy; that he may know that thy faithfulness is stronger than the cords of death.

" 'Let thy bowels also be full of charity towards all men, and to the household of faith, and let virtue garnish thy thoughts unceasingly; then shall thy confidence wax strong in the presence of God; and the doctrine of the priesthood shall distil upon thy soul as the dews from heaven. The Holy Ghost shall be thy constant companion, and thy scepter an unchanging scepter of righteousness and truth; and thy dominion shall be an everlasting dominion, and without compulsory means it shall flow unto thee forever and ever.' "[2]

The speaker read these solemn words with a clarion voice, causing them to resound through the thronged room. He read with impact and emphasis. He made the words seem wonderfully new, a refreshing revelation just announced, directly germane to home teaching in today's troubled world. When he was through, he lowered the booklet and studied again the variety of faces in the assembly.

"Brethren, what does it cost us to have the Holy Ghost as a companion? What price must we pay?" He paused, knowing no answer would be called out.

"Joseph Smith, in that same Liberty Jail revelation, wrote that the powers of heaven can only be controlled upon principles of righteousness, and that we cannot do so while covering our sins or gratifying our pride or our vain ambition, nor can we exercise authority over others.[3] So we discover that being a home teacher for Christ takes more than just dropping in once a month. It takes spirituality—as I believe we have unequivocally established—but it also takes other qualities: judgment, energy, integrity, courage, good manners, thoughtfulness. We could go on, but better still, let me illustrate how some of these qualities combine in an outstanding home teacher.

"I have been researching home teaching on assignment from the stake president, gathering facts and feelings from some of the Church members I know. One bishop related to me a home teaching situation in his ward that had caused him and others great distress. It seems that one of his young married couples, a couple he was just activating, had started shying away from attending their meetings, shunning him when they did come out. When he went to their home one night, when he sat and asked what was happening in their lives (for he had been preparing them for temple marriage), he was told by the tearful wife that she was appalled at the 'lack of feeling' expressed by the ward members and, to his greater surprise, by him, the bishop.

"He was personally dismayed at hearing this and pressed to find the reason for her frustration. He discovered that her sister, her only nearby relative, had recently died in a most painful and sudden manner—and no one in the ward had said a word in sympathy to her. She and her husband had mourned all alone, stood forlorn and painfully alone beside the casket on the night of the viewing. She was quite bitter about it. Where were the ward members? she asked. Where was the bishop? she lamented."

Brother Larrabee held up the committee's printed booklet once again, waving it as a signal. "Some of you may know that my own home teacher, Brother Crabtree sitting over there, baptized me several weeks back. And one of the things he and I did, in preparation for my becoming one of the 'fold of God,' was to review God's baptismal covenant.

"What did we all really agree to when we came into God's fold? into The Church of Jesus Christ of Latter-day Saints? I was much impressed with the baptismal covenant Brother Crabtree and I read together. I was warmed by it, heartened by it. I rejoiced in uniting with such a concerned and harmonious group of Christians, to join with them, the wonderful Mormons. But—the tearful wife in our little story, she may have once felt a close kinship to her ward family, yet now she was alienated from them. Why? Why was she feeling terribly let down?

"It was because no one in her ward—including the bishop—lived up to the baptismal covenant. That's where they failed her. I want to read that covenant to you now. It has been included in your booklet. In fact, it is also found in the Book of Mormon, but sometimes we glide right over it without feeling the power of this pledge, the unconditional adherence it cries out for."

Again he stopped pacing. Standing straight and tall he said, "I want to read it very slowly because of the impact of commitment these words carry, sacred words, words of seriousness and sanctity—words every Mormon ostensibly agreed to before being baptized. Simply stated, gentlemen," he said forthrightly, "this is a covenant, a contract, that binds us to God, that binds us to each other. The prophet Alma is speaking: 'Behold, here are the waters of Mormon (for thus were they called) and now, as ye are desirous to come into the fold of God, and to be called his people, and are willing to bear one another's burdens, that they may be light; yea, and are willing to mourn with those that mourn; yea, and comfort those that stand in need of comfort, and to stand as witnesses of God at all times and in all things, and in all places that ye may be in, even until death, that ye may be redeemed of God, and be numbered with those of the first resurrection, that ye may have eternal life — now I say unto you, if this be the desire of your hearts, what have you against being baptized in the name of the Lord, as a witness before him that ye have entered into a covenant with him, that ye will serve him and keep his commandments, that he may pour out his Spirit more abundantly upon you?'[4]

"You see, brethren, this young wife had waited for someone to come and help her bear her heavy burden, mourn with her over the sudden death of her dear sister, put an arm around her, support her in her grief. When no one came, she obviously felt she was outside the 'fold of God.' All she had in all of this great city to comfort her were her baby and her husband, the inactive, indifferent husband the bishop had been toiling with to kindle desires to be a better husband, to take her to the temple."

Brother Larrabee stared again at the covenant printed in the booklet, then dropped it on the table behind him. "But the bishop protested," he said, his voice rising. "He had not known of her dear sister's death. He surely would have come—as would the rest of the ward—if only they had known. Why hadn't she told him? told someone?

"And here she had him, for she looked up with tears swimming in her eyes and explained she had told someone. She had told her home teacher! She had told her friendly home teacher, she said, because she knew he represented the bishop when he came into her apartment. Telling the home teacher was like telling the bishop, she said. Yes, and now she did have the bishop, had him cold, left without excuse, as the scripture says."

Throwing up both hands in resignation, Brother Larrabee went on. "It didn't matter what protests the bishop made after that. Her bitterness was not ameliorated one bit when he attempted to explain his ignorance by repeating that the home teacher had not passed that important news on to him." Brother Larrabee lowered his voice and said confidingly: "Incidentally, she was right in her feelings that the home teacher would report the news of her tragedy to the bishop. Home teaching is a two-way communications conduit: messages should be carried back and forth by the home teacher. That is the Lord's program.

"I asked the bishop what followed that sorry scene. He nearly quoted me verbatim from that 'Guidelines for Home Teachers' I just read you, saying he had been so moved upon by the Spirit to reprove the offending home teacher with sharpness that he called him onto the carpet in the bishop's office and surprised himself with the vigor of his expressed feelings. And while showing forth an increase of love to the thoughtless elder afterward, the bishop decided that he wouldn't have him replaced as the weeping wife's home teacher, that even though there was obvious damage to their relationship, yet, maybe the best thing for the embittered couple and the home teacher was to continue that association with renewed concern, exploiting the unspent spirituality."

When he was making a major point, Brother Larrabee often rubbed his hands. He rubbed them now and said: "The bishop could hardly believe his ears when the same weeping wife called him on the phone two weeks later to report—directly to him—the sudden death of her baby. What? Another catastrophe? Yes, a double disaster. The baby's death now layered heavily, heartlessly, on top of the sister's passing.

"But this death was different. With full knowledge of the needs the young couple had, the bishop was able to use the marvelous resources of the entire ward to mourn, share burdens, give comfort. The rebirth of the home teacher was something to behold. He was the most earnest, the most considerate of all the ward members in supporting the weeping wife and her spiritually feeble husband. The home teacher was later to say he had never felt finer than the day of the burial when he stood beside the bishop at the graveside, stood there throughout the little service in a driving rainstorm, a heartless downpour. He claimed he came away soaked to the skin, had ruined his suit, and had been monumentally aglow with the Spirit.

"But that is not where the story ends," cautioned Brother Larrabee. "Although the repentant home teacher had performed well, yet there was an even more important role he was to take, voluntarily, and it occurred some days after the funeral.

"The weeping wife told the bishop that after all the crowds and comfort had drifted away, after funeral flowers had wilted and phone calls and visits had ceased, she and her husband sat in their tiny living room that next Saturday staring at the empty playpen and the vacant crib that had been such an important part of their little boy's life. And as they sat, they wondered out loud to each other if the gospel was really true. For if it was, they asked themselves, how could a loving Father have so cruelly stolen away—denied them—their sweet baby?

"They were at the breaking point. There was neither substance nor strength left in their faith.

"They were sitting there overwhelmed with their loss, numbed by the reality that their little boy was permanently gone. The high excitement and support that came with the funeral had floated off. They were alone and adrift, and their frail spiritual boat had a bad leak. They were slowly sinking, despairing, sitting there staring dully at the infant's empty furniture—when someone came up to their big window, peered in, waved, and walked right into their apartment without knocking.

"It was their home teacher," Brother Larrabee said exuberantly. "The penitent one, the one who'd sacrificed a suit in the rainstorm and felt uplifted by it. It was he who walked in smiling, waved, and started speaking pleasantly and encouragingly while taking several tools out of his pockets.

"All the time he was chatting, he was dismantling their baby's furniture, first the crib, then the playpen. He told the couple he'd been praying about them, about their sudden losses, about their lives and their faith and their need to stay closer to the Lord. He testified to them again and again that God lived—yes, and loved them. And all the time he was pleasantly working at his task. God loved them and had great things for them to accomplish, he said, if they only continued keeping faith and trust in the Lord.

"Their home teacher reiterated what they had heard during the small funeral about the plan of salvation and the eternal significance of the covenants and ordinances of holy temples that can bind families together. Finally, in a gesture reflecting his great sensitivity to them, he suggested that until the next child arrived, he would carry the playpen down to the apartment storage area. Brother Larrabee's eyes glistened. His face seemed lit from within.

"He filled them full of hope for the future, full of appreciation for the past, for their splendid little boy—so very special to God. He asked if he might be voice to their family prayer. (They had not prayed since the baby's death.) He knelt with them, the three of them holding hands as families sometimes do, and thanked the Lord for their blessings.

"This insightful home teacher was so vivid in his vision of their future, he was so profound in his expressions of gratitude for the goodness of God in their lives, for their little angel, for their fine marriage, their home, their health, their hopes, that they too began to see life renewed through his vision. He got them excited about going to the temple and having the little boy sealed to them as an eternal family. He carried away the baby's furniture, but he came back again and again, came back into that home and taught them more about God's great plan of salvation."

Brother Larrabee rubbed his hands. "The bishop concluded by saying that this one home teacher—who had failed once—completely turned the young couple's lives around. When they went to the temple, it was he, the home teacher, who knelt at the altar representing their son. When the new baby was born, another boy, it was given the home teacher's name. Yes, and it was that same home teacher who without being asked went down into the basement storeroom and retrieved the crib—and pleasantly rehearsed with the couple that Heavenly Father had certainly been swift in answering their prayers—all while he reassembled it."

He held both hands outstretched, imploringly. "Brethren, brethren, that is home teaching! That is what it's all about. That is the spirit of the gospel. That is compassion. That is Christlike service to others. That is stewardship in its richest form." He lowered his arms. "And though there will never be a manual written that dictates the broad variety of options home teachers might exercise in life's multitudinous situations, yet still the Spirit can lead you. The Spirit can direct honest, searching home teachers. And that is what the Lord wants for his home teachers—to be led by the Spirit."

His arms hung down, he bowed his head slightly and concluded by saying: "That is my testimony. That is what I have learned and absorbed and retained while serving on this marvelous committee, led by a president who himself is guided and inspired by the Spirit of the Lord."

Notes

1. Chapin Collins in the Montesano, Washington, *Vidette.*
2. D&C 121:41–46.
3. See D&C 121:36–37.
4. Mosiah 18:8–10.

7

Home Teaching—a Serious Business

Brother Larrabee had concluded his presentation, and the president immediately introduced the next speaker. This was Brother Wheeler, a high councilor also on the home teaching committee sitting in the front row. The president put an arm around him and warmly pointed out to the assembled priesthood leaders that not every high council in the Church was blessed with a man of Brother Wheeler's background—a bishop, a Ph.D. in clinical psychology, a department head at the local university, and a writer producing weekly columns on family relations in the metropolitan paper.

"Thank you, president, not just for this assignment to speak tonight," Brother Wheeler said looking down at the men seated on front row, "but for allowing me to serve on a most entertaining and provocative committee. I've thoroughly enjoyed all our sessions." Then looking up at the sea of faces, he said: "Brethren, we have been anxiously engaged in a grand engineering project: plumbing the depths and dimensions, testing the productive alignment, determining the widths and weaknesses in this stake's home teaching program. Does it hold water? Are there leaks?" He paused, smiling. "We have made the measure and decided we are doing only a fair job. Extended possibilities are bottomless."

He spoke as he wrote—witty and wordy.

"Hammering on home teaching carried me back to my calling as an elders quorum president. We set up a grand home teaching organization. It looked like a Jell-O mold—colorful and shimmering—that is, until things warmed up and we had a meltdown. Try as we might, our home teaching slowly softened. We never could firm it up, get any solid support. When I was finally released, the stake president back in those days asked me my feelings. I told him that I felt much like Senator Adlai Stevenson after his second defeat in running for president of the United States: 'I'm too old to cry, and it hurts too much to laugh.'

"Brethren, home teaching is a *serious* business. We represent the Lord to our assigned families. I didn't really understand that until later when I became counselor to an especially wise bishop. He was so dedicated to having a strong home teaching program that we all used to joke about it. We privately called his frenetic executive secretary 'Fang.' There was a fierce determination from the bishop and Fang to get good home teaching done at all cost.

"In a quiet moment alone, I gently chided the bishop. I told him he made it sound as though home teaching was a matter of life or death. He looked at me a long time and replied, 'Oh, no, it's much more important than that.' "

The speaker's eye rested on a very youthful quorum president, and he added: "This bishop was a spiritual colossus in my young life. I have many fond memories of those great learning years.

"It has been special these past weeks to work so closely with our inspired stake president. I enjoyed Brother Larrabee's poignant story about the little boy confusing General Sherman with his horse.

"That little boy reminded me of an occasion when a similar misunderstanding in communication occurred. I had built our family home evening around a little cardboard sign that read: 'I belong to a family that loves me.' I had each of our children hold it while we talked about him or her. Then we taped it to the refrigerator door for a month or so. During that period one of my daughter's friends asked her privately: 'Sarah, why does your family love that refrigerator so much?' "

The audience laughed appreciatively; the brethren were with him.

"I liked what Brother Larrabee said about the imperative of having the Holy Ghost as a companion when we home teach. Being guided by the Spirit, wouldn't that be a marvelous way to run our workaday lives? At one of our committee meetings discussing spirituality, I mentioned a curious spiritual message delivered to a mission president by an apostle when I was a young missionary. Our stake president has asked that I share it with you all tonight because it deals with being led by the Spirit. But before I do, let me tell you a little more about the apostle. Matthew Cowley was one of the great Church leaders who came into our mission. We hung on his every word. He had a lively sense of humor and a profound testimony of the gospel.

"During his visit to our mission headquarters, Brother Cowley was invited to speak at the Rotary Club luncheon. The mission president reported to us later that his talk on Mormon welfare was so amusing, so enthusiastically received by the Rotarians, that many of them crowded around him in the hotel lobby afterward, lingering to catch his parting words and to offer their congratulations. This included a local politician, a Rotary officer who had sat next to our apostle at the head table during the lunch. He had become a bit weary of remaining silent while all this attention was being heaped on Brother Cowley, so he decided to establish his own brand of humor. He stepped up to the apostle during his thronged parting and said, 'Mister Cowley, tell us before you leave, how does it feel to be a Mormon and know you're going to hell?'

"This was said in high good humor, you understand, though some of the Rotarians were shocked. But the apostle had them all whooping when he immediately grinned, a twinkle in his eye, and replied: 'First, sir, you must tell us how it feels to be a politician and not know where in hell you are going!' "

Brother Wheeler kept a straight face until it was quiet.

"Not everyone," he said in a more serious voice, "can dish out humor without offending people. Matthew Cowley was a master at it. But as a psychologist, I'd like to make this first point in my comments tonight—that humor is negative. Nearly always. This means that every time a joke is made, someone or something is usually being made fun of. Somewhere someone gets lampooned and hurt.

"On the other hand, Christ's gospel is totally positive. And because his plan of salvation is so very serious, you will not find anything humorous or foolish in the scriptures. And you won't find it in the temples or the solemn assemblies or other sacred places. The Lord counsels us to avoid loud laughter and being light-minded about sacred things. The work of the Lord is holy. Holiness is serious.

"Life and death? No, teaching the gospel is much more important than that." He leaned back against the big table. "So the first point I'd like to make tonight is that humor—warming, uplifting humor—can be extremely helpful in getting close to people. But," and Brother Wheeler held up his hand, palm out like the traffic policeman, "humor must be used selectively, carefully. Effective humor calls for judgment and good taste."

He folded his arms and smiled. "You see, my wonderful bishop had great balance in his dealing with people. Like Matthew Cowley, he used humor well. He could easily laugh at his executive secretary being called Fang because he knew his man, knew Fang enjoyed the name and notoriety. Fang was laughing too.

"But let's get back to Matthew Cowley, the apostle. The meat of my message about him occurred the day after his Rotary talk, when he was about to leave the mission home. We were standing on the wide veranda, he and the president. I was there, having just put his suitcase in the waiting car. He had set my new mission president apart that very morning, and the president was concerned over not having some important questions answered. You see, this assignment to preside had come only recently, unexpectedly. He and his wife were originally called as proselyting missionaries. Then our original president became ill and was rushed home, and now Brother Cowley had come out, given the new president his calling and setting apart, and was himself rushing off.

"So the new president inquired anxiously of the departing apostle if there weren't some special instructions he was yet to receive.

" 'Instructions?' the apostle asked, puzzled. 'Why, yes,' my mission president stammered. 'Aren't you going to give me some specific counsel on what I must do to be the mission president? Aren't there some important things I should know?'

"The apostle smiled benevolently, smiled even as he signaled the driver that he was coming. 'Oh, yes, forgive me. I forgot. I will give you the same counsel President Heber J. Grant gave me after ordaining me an apostle and then announcing he was hurrying off to lunch before the next session of conference. I was thunderstruck by all that had just happened and asked him your very question: Weren't there some special, secret instructions I must be given to function as a new member of the Council of the Twelve? President Grant paused at the door, thanked me for asking, then instructed me to wear long socks and to be sure I pulled them up straight before sitting on the stand at stake conferences. Long socks? Yes, he said, explaining that if I wore those little half socks, the congregation would see my naked calf when I crossed my legs. That would not be dignified for a member of the Twelve, he told me—and he hurried out of the temple rooms.'

"My new mission president and I were both bewildered at this answer. But the apostle threw us a wave and a fleeting smile, hurried down the porch steps, and jumped into the car.

"I had to wait until the next day to ask my president what that meant, the strange message about pulling up socks. He seemed remarkably improved and relieved from the day before. I thought he had seemed to be in pain as we watched the car carry off the only man around with the authority to enlighten him. And my new president admitted as much, for he confided to me that he had certainly felt abandoned.

"He said he was forced into spending much of that night praying and searching the scriptures. And only then did the full weight of Matthew Cowley's message hit him. He had discovered for himself, come to realize that instructions for mission presidents and apostles were to be found by searching the scriptures, by praying and pondering, by seeking the Spirit, by getting closer to God!"

Brother Wheeler, the astute academic doctor of clinical psychology, said with emphasis, "My new president had discovered overnight that the secret to good human relations was to be found in praying and in searching out and pondering the word of the Lord."

He now turned, reached over to the pile of pamphlets, the new home teaching booklet, and picked one up.

"That is not only true for apostles and mission presidents but also for bishops, quorum leaders, and—home teachers. The Lord governs his church through the whisperings of the Spirit, inspiring anxious and responsible leaders. As for home teachers, there is no manual big enough to cover all the spiritual problems one pair of home teachers might uncover in providing a true stewardship over their little handful of assigned souls."

He peered down again at the task committee in front of him. "So my second point is that this committee our stake president called together is in total agreement that the Spirit is the best guide for divinely directing home teachers. This little booklet we are introducing to you merely contains a few scriptural guidelines, some listings and other how-to counsel to direct home teachers into doing exactly what President Heber J. Grant said—which was, I think, to pull up your socks and lean on the Spirit. Grand counsel in human relations."

He touched his fingertips to his lower lip, reflecting.

"I like that," he said and repeated it softly: "Pull up your socks and lean on the Spirit." He opened the booklet and leafed through several pages.

"Let me get into the booklet now, but not without sharing with you some painful comments about home teaching from one of my co-workers. As our stake president has said, I am on the university faculty. There is only one other Mormon in my department. When she learned I was putting some materials together for home teaching she said, 'Oh, dear, I wish someone would take our home teacher aside and tell him how weary we've become of his forever using our living room as a forum to vent his strong personal feelings about things. They are almost always about empty things, things that have no meaning for me and my family but are important to him. He has really become an embarrassment. But how do we switch him to another channel?'

"Mark her use of the word 'empty,' brethren. Because one of the first things you will find in your copy of our booklet is this quotation from a General Authority who is also apprehensive about empty home teaching." And Brother Wheeler opened the booklet and read: 'To make the gospel effective . . . home teaching is really intended to be the vehicle by which the gospel will be administered to members of the Church. Most home teachers either do not go or they go empty—that means their vehicle is either broken or it is unloaded. I think you have all seen those empty pickup trucks running around the ward in great profusion.'[1]

"My associate at the university has her home teachers coming regularly. That's wonderful! But then she says they deliver an empty load. They say little that is uplifting or has application for her family. They are confusing activity with accuracy. They are driving over to her house every month, but they're bringing nothing in their pickup. And why is that? Perhaps it is because they lack the simple skills in discovering the needs of others."

Brother Wheeler tugged at his chin again. "Let me make my next point out of our booklet by asking some questions. Which of you, as a home teacher, can say that someone over whom you have a priesthood stewardship doesn't seriously need counsel and encouragement, need someone to talk to, a nonjudgmental listener, someone to rejoice with and share deep feelings? How can you know? How can you be sure—unless you have asked them?

"Brethren, you are all home teachers. Are you asking questions to discover what's best to teach? or how to help? Are you seeking specific answers for your families? Are you prayerfully offering your support? When did you last do something for your family other than sit on their couch and talk about some abstract subject of your choice? Worse still, do you have any idea what they think of your visits? Isn't that a threatening thing to consider? Just ask yourself: What might they tell their friends privately about me, about my performance?"

He stopped completely and stuffed his hands deep in his pockets.

"Perhaps one of you out there is the home teacher that disappoints my department associate—because she lives in this stake!" Then he lowered his voice and added: "And if it isn't you, then it's someone you supervise. How can you find him? How can you help him? For that is your job—helping home teachers. And let me say it loud and clear: Learning what people feel means asking questions and listening with sensitivity.

"But let's talk about your families. I ask you this: Is your spiritual vision so clouded by the cataract of indifference that you cannot recognize and identify the needs of others? so you cannot help them? support them? Even the Savior himself, as a mortal, needed comfort and, indeed, received it from angels that were sent to visit him for that very purpose.[2] Are you really confident you are comforting people? confident you are doing a good job as a home teacher?" He frowned and sniffed. "I had a distressed patient tell me the other day that confidence was the feeling he had before he understood the problem.

"Permit me," Brother Wheeler continued, "to use a little humor now, whimsey to illustrate a vital point in human relations. It demonstrates one of the most important sources of confusion between people. In my story, a woman goes to her attorney and explains that she would like a divorce. He asks if she has grounds. 'Yes,' she says, 'we have two acres.' 'No, no, do you have a grudge?' 'No,' she answers, 'we have a carport.' The lawyer casts about for another opening and finally asks if her husband beats her up. 'Oh, no,' she replies, 'I'm usually starting breakfast even before he is awake.' Thoroughly frustrated, the lawyer inquires if she is serious about wanting a divorce. 'Actually, I don't want one,' she mutters. 'It's my husband's idea. He claims we don't communicate.'

"So communication is the key to good human relations. And listening is the lever to opening that door. Listen, then, while I read to you a list of eight guidelines you will find in your booklet."

Eight Keys in Communicating

1. *Ask questions.* You cannot know the family's needs unless you ask appropriate questions and listen carefully to their answers.

2. *Concentrate on what they say.* Too many times we merely pretend to listen, waiting for that moment when we can jump back in and take control of the conversation. Listen intently. Soak up what they are saying.

3. *Repeat back what they have just said.* When it is appropriate for you to respond, do so by repeating the essence of what they have just told you, for example, "Then you believe that . . . " And so on. This lets them know you have heard what they said. It gives them a chance to continue talking. They know you are listening.

4. *Do not change the subject.* Stay with what they are telling you. When they are quite finished, help them to continue talking by asking another related question.

5. *Invite them to tell you more.* If what they are saying is productive to you, encourage them to continue: "Tell me more . . . What else did you feel? . . . Then what did you say?"

6. *Do not interrupt.* When you force yourself into their monologue, it obviously breaks into their line of thought. Depending on how forceful or oblique your interruption is, they may never return to the genuine feelings they were trying to communicate to you.

7. *Do not let them see you are not interested.* If they lose eye contact with you because you are gazing about, looking through your scriptures, moving and shifting

your position, they will quickly recognize you are not listening to them, not interested in what they are saying. Their words may, in fact, be uninteresting—but even so, your concentration and sensitivity about what they are saying will help you learn more of them and thus become a more helpful home teacher.

8. *Avoid criticism.* How can you be a helpful sounding board if you are too quick to criticize or too vocal in your evaluation? Take a soft approach. Compliment the family where you can. If they see you as being reasonable and responsive, they will seek your counsel and advice again and again. Avoiding criticism builds a trusting relationship!

Brother Wheeler stopped reading and grimaced. "This little booklet has many lists of things home teachers might wish to repeatedly consider and review. And I want to make a big point of this, because someone is bound to say lists are sophomoric and unnecessary. Nonsense! Lists are productive. They can be extremely helpful. The Lord himself uses lists. We have ten commandments, thirteen articles of faith. Bible scholars have labeled the beatitudes as 'nine declarations of supreme blessedness.' "

He pointed into the crowd: "You bishops have a specific list of printed questions to ask every temple-recommend applicant. And if anything on that list puts someone on a guilt trip, then it has served its purpose, and you have an excellent opportunity to discuss his or her problem.

"I learned in the mission field," the high councilor continued, "to make lists for my self-improvement, writing down my goals, making daily entries in my journal—a list of my activities and feelings. Some years ago I clipped an item from *Newsweek* magazine about a popular Mormon golfer and the little lists he made for himself. We didn't put this in your home teaching booklet, but let me read it to you now:

" 'Johnny Miller, 27, the first professional golfer ever to win the first three tournaments of any year (which he did this year), thinks a golfer's best game is in his head, and he takes great pains to record every nuance of the sport. He carries around an old brown envelope on which he jots down little reminders to himself: Take the club back slowly . . . You must keep the head still . . . Make sure you are comfortable before starting the swing.

" 'Miller readily admits that all this sounds corny but, he says, I believe the brain is a computer. If you keep feeding things into it, it remembers and transfers them to the body. That's why all the sayings are positive. Actually, they're commands.' " Brother Wheeler mused over the clipping then held it up for all to see.

"But you don't need to make a list of little reminders on how to be a better home teacher, not on a brown envelope. They are already printed in our booklet. They may not seem important at first glance, but they are basic—and powerful. Any earnest priesthood holder can improve his performance. As Johnny Miller says, our best game may be in our head.

"As early as 1832, Joseph Smith received the important revelation he chose to call the 'Olive Leaf . . . plucked from the Tree of Paradise.'[3] In this revelation, the Lord tells us we must 'testify and warn the people . . . therefore, they are left without excuse . . . ' and to 'be perfect in your ministry . . . to prepare the saints for the hour of judgment which is to come.'[4]

"There it is! Your instruction from the Lord on how to home teach involves preparation. You are to prepare the Saints—your home teaching families—for the judgment which is to come. Brethren! Being able to *teach* preparation *requires* preparation—and preparation calls for training. And training is what our little booklet is all about, simple as our lists might seem."

Having said this, Brother Wheeler lifted up a visual aid on the table behind him and read it slowly and loudly:

" 'Training Is Everything.

" 'The peach was once a bitter almond; cauliflower is nothing but cabbage with a college education.'[5]

"Brethren, this folksy endorsement of training was made by a man born just three years after Joseph Smith received that revelation on preparation. This man was destined to be a simple printer on the Missouri frontier—until he trained himself as a writer. A great writer. A world-class writer. Every one of us in this room has at some time read and been stirred by the powerful, glowing prose of the man whose pen name was Mark Twain.

"His philosophy was simple. He believed that a human being is the product of two factors: heredity and training. He said, 'Since heredity cannot be altered after the fact, training is the only important variable in human success.'[6] Thus, training for Mark Twain, this towering literary genius, was everything. It is true he did not understand the workings of the Holy Ghost or that 'the Spirit of Christ is given to every man,'[7] and he certainly didn't know how to pull up his socks and seek the Spirit. But he did know that training is the key to preparation. And in that he was right.

"Permit me now to read quickly through the ten governing rules for home teachers. Later on you can read these in your booklet and study them and pray about them and absorb the training they can teach you."

Ten Governing Rules for Home Teachers

1. Make your visits prayerfully. You are on the Lord's errand. Pray for his help and direction. Always pray in the home if agreeable to the family.

2. Prepare your companionship for the visit: have a goal and a plan.

3. Be kind and encouraging during your visit. Praise whenever possible.

4. Show sincere interest in the family you visit. Rejoice, weep, mourn, console, enjoy. Concentrate on them, on their needs.

5. Be constantly cheerful and uplifting. Do not drag in your own burdens. Do not dwell on your aches and pains. Do not exploit the triumphs and tragedies of your life, great though they might be.

6. Remember you represent the Savior. It's his gospel you are teaching. Do and say what you feel he would have you do and say.

7. "Let virtue garnish thy thoughts unceasingly." Never speak ill of others, of righteous programs and policies, of the Lord's anointed leaders.

8. Search out and tenderly consider the family's feelings. You are in their home to identify their needs, to teach and prepare them in righteousness.

9. Radiate genuine humility. The Savior never boasted or bragged. For all he achieved—and he created everything that was created—he was humble. He gave all credit to the Father.

10. Bear a strong testimony during each visit. Testify of Christ's example, his gospel, his scriptures, his church, his leaders, his programs.

With the booklet still open in his hands, Brother Wheeler continued, "Right after these ten governing rules, we have included an interesting item we found in the *Church News*. Since it told of the successful activation of a couple by their home teachers, specifically citing the effective exercise of three of our ten governing rules, we have included it in the booklet as follows:

Three Things Home Teachers Did That Activated Us

When the home teachers came to our home for the first time, we expected a long lesson or sermon about our inactivity in the Church. We were very surprised to find it a friendly visit with:

> 1. A sincere concern for us and our family. After a few short months we felt free to discuss any of our problems with them and knew that we would receive a helpful answer.
>
> 2. The strong testimony our home teachers bore to us made us know that the Church is true and that it is important for us to put forth a special effort to better ourselves.
>
> 3. We were quite surprised when our home teachers asked us if we would join with them in prayer. Those prayers were always in our behalf and just what we needed.[8]

Brother Wheeler patted the next page. "Now, take a minute and consider this question: What are the little things active home teachers do that irritate their families? We took a survey right in this stake, and we identified seven things concerned home teachers should never do. These too are in your booklet, and I shall read them to you now. Listen and ponder—yes, and ask yourself if you are guilty of some of these."

Seven Things Home Teachers Should Never Do

- Never just drop in unannounced.
- Never use the family as a captive audience for your ego.
- Never talk of things that interest only you.
- Never ask embarrassing questions.
- Never dominate the discussion.
- Never stay too long.
- Never encourage negative remarks.

The presenting high councilor read all of the above without departing, and he testified that these suggestions, the essence of lengthy discussions by the stake committee, could also be added upon—increased or decreased—as the Spirit directed. But the basic seven, he said, should be considered as training helps, guidelines, to expand effectiveness in the home teacher's determination to improve himself.

"Now, my brethren, priesthood leaders of our great stake, I come to a very exciting part of my presentation, a few comments about people and personality styles and what makes us different.

"Right now our best ethnological researchers estimate there are over five billion people living in the world. That simply means there are over five billion differing personalities. No two people are identical or have equivalent feelings at all times. President Kimball used to talk about the genealogy load the Church must work through, and stated on several occasions that there have been sixty-nine billion people who have lived on the earth since Adam's day. To the functioning clinical psychologist, that means sixty-nine billion personalities deviating in sixty-nine billion heterogeneous directions.

"People can be broadly categorized, broken down into galaxies of homogeneous groupings. That helps academicians organize an understanding of our fellow humans. But even in using the broadest of brush strokes, personality styles are terribly complex, difficult for the best trained professionals to understand. Then what about home teachers and their understanding of their assigned families?

"You are certainly not going into psychoanalysis, let alone psychotherapy. But it is important that you open your minds to the simple fact that people are different, vastly different. You cannot present an identical message to four dissimilar families and have four identical responses. No, they each respond differentially as families, and divergently as individuals within the family.

"People differ drastically in age. And that too affects their needs. During a home teaching visit, you sit there facing babes in arms, grandparents, teenagers, young marrieds: a big demographic mishmash waiting to hear what you have prepared for them. And let me remind you again that a person who is single is considered a family unit on Church records. How is it possible to accommodate all these age groups and circumstances with one message?

"But allow me to pause on the age factor for a minute. Just because a person is old does not mean he or she is too old to be instructed, to be encouraged to change, to improve, to be better prepared in something. What on earth is 'too old'? Moses was eighty when he led the Twelve Tribes out of Egypt. Benjamin Franklin helped frame the United States Constitution at eighty-one. Golda Meir became prime minister of Israel at seventy-one. Lorenzo Snow was shocked when the Lord called on him to become president of the Church at eighty-four, but Ezra Taft Benson became president at eighty-six. George Bernard Shaw wrote and produced a great play at ninety-four. Many professional athletes drop out in their early thirties, but the legendary Ted Williams slammed a home run in his last official time at bat—at the remarkable age of forty-two.

"As for the youthful side of mortality, what is 'too young'? Joseph Smith was fourteen when he was given the most astonishing of all commissions. William Pitt was twenty-four when he became prime minister of Great Britain. Benjamin Franklin was an established newspaper columnist at sixteen. Joseph F. Smith was sixteen when called on his first mission. Mozart was just seven when his first composition was published. And Mickey Mantle hit twenty-three home runs his first year in the major leagues—at age twenty.

"But let's stay with my subject of people and personalities. I do some consulting work for a national corporation. To aid their sales force, they have attempted to classify all prospective customers into four basic personality groups. This was done for a wisely calculated reason, because if a salesman can identify the individuality of the person he is trying to sell—why, he has a major advantage.

"These four behavioral profiles have been developed and classified by psychologists through empirical research, that is, gained from observation or experimentation rather than theorized. The profiles are labeled as (1) the pragmatic personality, (2) the analytical personality, (3) the amiable personality, and (4) the extrovert."

Brother Wheeler came to a full stop, put on his most serious face, and, shaking his head, said: "Now let me make my point. It is this—that scientists can put together, in layman's terms, a focused description of basic personalities that has commercial value to those who are willing to study and memorize such material. But—and this is the point—this information will never be as useful in understanding people as will seeking the Spirit and the power of discernment.

"And as a psychologist I can tell you that the best thing I've heard about understanding people is God's counsel that we be willing to 'bear one another's burdens.'

"There was another reason for my exercise in sharing with you those four personality sketches. It is to open up our minds to the fact that a lot of work has been done in the world to understand the complexities of our fellow mortals. But the Lord says it best: 'Succor the weak, lift up the hands which hang down, and strengthen the feeble knees.'[9] No, brethren, I know of no group that has your stability, your grasp of life and its meaning.

"What does the world know of the workings of the Spirit? Those of you who love George Frederic Handel's ultimate triumph, his immortal choral music, *Messiah,* may be familiar with the fact that he composed this towering work—four hours of sublime chorals, solos, and orchestrations—in just twenty-four days. We believe he was inspired of the Lord. He said he had 'companionship of the Spirit.'

Recently some psychiatrists presented a more worldly answer to that divine influence. They claimed he suffered from a mood disorder, that he was a manic depressive, that he wrote his masterpiece during an intense psychotic change of disposition. He hallucinated!"

He took a paper from his coat pocket and unfolded it. "I was reading just the other night a serious essay by a man who has won the Pulitzer Prize for his writing and his wisdom. He states, 'The human soul is a house of many fantastic chambers.' Then he asks a touching question: 'What ruled this curious thing called human existence?—what forces swayed it most wholly and made it pageant or tragedy or only gray succession of lackluster days?'[10]

"He asks his question but has no answer. Just think how you and your testimony of Christ could bring light into his life. Think what a pair of dedicated home teachers could teach him if he would listen.

"One parting comment," Brother Wheeler said in a quiet voice, leaning back against the big table and folding up the paper. "It is about a Harvard professor of neuropathology, a Dr. Murray who in the late thirties reasoned that since the study of mental illness always involved neurotic and psychopathic people, he would launch a study of people who were mentally healthy. He wanted to learn what made healthy people so well-adjusted. At first, he used Harvard students, but he discovered to his amazement that they all had hidden symptoms of mental distress—though they were performing normally.

"He next studied healthy blue-collar workers and discovered the same thing. They each showed latent signs of serious mental problems but gave no evidence of it in their activities. So it was that he moved from one group to another until he was able to externalize for us this amazing conclusion—that all healthy people have concealed mental problems that they keep under control!

"Now here comes the kicker. From Dr. Murray's research, we can make an interesting analogy: that from birth each of us carries congenital mental weaknesses, which can be likened to a bag of rocks. And as we stumble through life, some of us can handle our big bag and some of us cannot. Some are overcome, overburdened, and drop the bag, or lose some or all of the rocks, or fall off life's twisting course desperately clutching their load while trying to keep their balance. Those are the people that need various degrees of encouragement, or even professional mental help, or serious medical help. But the point Dr. Murray makes is that every mortal, every one of us, carries a heavy load through life.

"And I say to you, brethren, that this being true—and I believe it is—it is vital that we look about us, at ourselves and our loved ones, at our assigned home teaching families, and remember that each person needs our persuasion, our teaching, our testimony, our help."

Brother Wheeler suddenly seemed drained of energy. He had given them much to think upon. But he held up his traffic policeman's hand for one last word.

"You don't need a Ph.D. in anything to be an earnest, humble, effective home teacher. What you need is the Spirit. I leave you with the most powerful counsel I could possibly give, the sure word of the Lord from the scriptures, saying: 'The elders, priests and teachers of this church shall teach the principles of my gospel, which are in the Bible and the Book of Mormon, in the which is the fulness of the gospel. And they shall observe the covenants and church articles to do them, and these shall be their teachings, as they shall be directed by the Spirit. And the Spirit shall be given unto you by the prayer of faith.' "[11]

Notes

1. W. Grant Bangerter, First Quorum of Seventy meeting, September 27, 1979.
2. Matthew 4:11.

3. *History of the Church,* 1:302–12.
4. D&C 88:81–84.
5. Mark Twain, *Pudd'nhead Wilson.*
6. Nightingale Conant Publications, October 1989.
7. Mormon 7:16.
8. *Church News,* March 25, 1967.
9. D&C 81:5.
10. "Elementals," by Stephen Vincent Benet.
11. D&C 42:12–14.

8

The Effective Home Teacher

"As I have told you before, in this stake it had better be an unusually good meeting to be better than no meeting at all." The stake president said this after thanking Brother Wheeler for his words and testimony. "And I firmly believe this has been a great meeting thus far, thanks to Brothers Larrabee and Wheeler. And you will appreciate it even more when you take home the booklets that we have just passed out to you.

"Please turn to page 6 in your booklet and let us examine this overview of the Church: The mission of the Church is to bring souls to Christ. This is accomplished by (1) proclaiming the gospel—worldwide missionary work, (2) perfecting the Saints—progress for the living, and (3) redeeming the dead—family history and temple work.

"As a committee studying home teaching, we are especially focused on the second one, perfecting the Saints, which includes an emphasis on spiritual and temporal welfare. When asked during our first committee meeting, Brother Larrabee admitted that most well-functioning organizations today develop a mission statement, adopting it as a transcending guide or goal or vision.

"We took up this challenge for home teaching, searching the scriptures and reviewing statements made by contemporary prophets and apostles. I would like you now to continue with me down the page as I read this inspiring statement giving a home teacher the consummate purpose and direction for his labors:

" 'A Mission Statement for Home Teachers

" 'Home teaching, properly functioning, brings to the house of each member two priesthood bearers divinely commissioned and authoritatively called into the service by their priesthood leader and bishop. These home teachers—priesthood bearers—carry the heavy and glorious responsibility of representing the Lord Jesus Christ in looking after the welfare of each Church member. They are to encourage and inspire every member to discharge his duty to both family and church.'[1]

"That statement was made by Marion G. Romney of the First Presidency a few years back. Nothing has been altered since he gave the Church that vision of the sacred mission of home teachers. We prayerfully gathered together a wealth of wonderful statements and felt this one said it best.

"I endorse all that the two brethren who spoke before me have said about the companionship of the Holy Ghost and about truly representing our Lord Jesus Christ. Solemn thoughts." He stood silent, gazing down at the booklet in his hand.

"Solemn thoughts indeed," he echoed. This was a man they could follow. This was a man—their president—with a testimony that touched them. He could not mention the Savior's name without being moved by it, by the sacredness of it, and without moving others.

"We have set up for ourselves the sober task of profiling the effective home teacher," he continued. "What does he do? What does he teach? What does he look for as he holds stewardship over his little flock? How does he represent his quorum leader, his bishop, and the Savior?

"Let us first read the scripture that precedes that profile:

" 'Wherefore, now let every man learn his duty, and to act in the office in which he is appointed, in all diligence.'[2]

"This booklet, with its many statements and scriptures and lists, is a collection of what we believe the Lord wants each home teacher to know if he is willing to 'learn his duty.' And, incidentally," the president said, looking up, "the verse that follows carries a powerful warning for those of us who aren't interested: 'He that is slothful shall not be counted worthy to stand.'

"Dear brethren, we need to learn our duty as home teachers and to act and perform with full vigor, vitality, and commitment. But there is a difference between responsibility and duty. Those of us who have served in the military understand that difference. You might shirk your responsibility, but you have no options with duty. Duty is firmly outlined, described, dictated to the serviceman. It is not an assignment he can dodge. It is a duty that must be done, first and foremost. In the military, duty has fierce penalties for failure to perform. It is the same in the army of the Lord.

"What we have done to outline duties for home teachers is to carefully collate and critically compare key scriptures that describe priesthood duties, such as the following."

Key Scriptures That Define Duties for Home Teachers

> Trust no one to be your teacher nor your minister, except he be a man of God, walking in his ways and keeping his commandments . . . and none were consecrated except they were just men. Therefore they did watch over their people, and did nourish them with things pertaining to righteousness. (Mosiah 23:14, 17, 18.)
>
> Remember in all things the poor and the needy, the sick and the afflicted, for he that doeth not these things, the same is not my disciple. (D&C 52:40.)
>
> The teacher's duty is to watch over the church al-

> ways, and be with and strengthen them; and see that there is no iniquity in the church, neither hardness with each other, neither lying, backbiting, nor evil speaking; and see that the church meet together often, and also see that all the members do their duty. (D&C 20:53–55.)
>
> The high priest and the elder are to administer in spiritual things, agreeable to the covenants and commandments of the church. (D&C 107:12.)
>
> Verily I say, men should be anxiously engaged in a good cause, and do many things of their own free will, and bring to pass much righteousness; for the power is in them, wherein they are agents unto themselves. And inasmuch as men do good they shall in nowise lose their reward. (D&C 58:26–27.)
>
> The deacons and teachers should be appointed to watch over the church, to be standing ministers unto the church. (D&C 84:111.)

"Now, my brethren," the president said after reading these several scriptures, "we have developed an outline from those verses that highlight qualities necessary in a home teacher." And again he read to them as they followed:

Scripturally Defined Qualities of a Dutiful Home Teacher

1. Must be a man of God.
2. Walking in his ways.
3. Keeping his commandments.
4. Must receive the authority to preach and teach.
5. Must be a just man.
6. Must watch over the people (as assigned).
7. Nourishing them pertaining to righteousness.
8. Strengthening them.
9. Remembering the poor and needy.
10. Remembering the sick and afflicted.
11. Seeing there is no iniquity.
12. Seeing there is no hardness with each other.
13. Seeing there is no lying or backbiting.

14. Seeing there is no evil speaking.
15. Seeing they meet together often.
16. Seeing all members do their duty.
17. Willing to administer in spiritual things.
18. Willing to do many good things without being commanded.
19. Willing to be standing ministers.

"Brethren, I hope you appreciate that the Lord has said so very much, and in so very many places. We have merely organized it in a helpful outline form. And you'll note that next we have taken up that final point about being a standing minister. What is a standing minister? The wordmasters on our committee checked their lexicons and have attempted to define the term as follows."

Definitions of a Standing Minister

1. One who has status with respect to his reputation and esteem.
2. One who is permanent and unchanging.
3. One who is not moving, but stationary.

"For many years I have kept a quotation of Benjamin Disraeli framed in my office at work. He was prime minister of England when he said it a century ago, but he might have made a great standing minister in the Lord's home teaching program today. He said, 'The secret of success is constancy of purpose.' That is what the standing minister represents to me, a home teacher who is always there, going into the homes of his families with 'constancy of purpose' until he is released.

"So let us now turn the page. We have discussed the difference between duty and responsibility, duty being mandated, duty meaning we *must* watch over our families by visiting in their homes. But responsibility is oftentimes shirked. We might visit in the home, doing our duty, but as Brother Wheeler said, drive in with an empty load.

Responsibility involves stewardship and accountability. It relates to 'how,' not 'whether or not' we do our duty.

"In striving to organize so many facets of home teaching, we have included thirteen of the basic responsibilities a home teacher should acknowledge in doing his duty." The president looked up once more. "And be assured, brethren, that you may add a great many more responsibilities as the Spirit moves you in serving your own families. But we feel these thirteen are essential."

Thirteen Fundamental Responsibilities of Home Teachers

1. Live to enjoy the companionship of the Holy Ghost and act under his influence as a home teacher.
2. Encourage the parents to whom you have assignment to obtain the blessings of the temple.
3. Encourage children not born under the covenant to be sealed to their parents.
4. Encourage unmarried members to set goals for missionary service and temple marriage.
5. Encourage family prayers night and morning.
6. Encourage consistent personal prayer.
7. Teach other gospel doctrine and standards and encourage their personal application.
8. Encourage regular family home evenings.
9. Teach that children should be blessed and baptized in harmony with Church revelations.
10. Teach that ordinations in the priesthood are merited and obtained in proper season.
11. Persuade priesthood bearers to attend their priesthood meetings and meet assigned obligations.
12. Persuade each member to attend sacrament meetings.
13. Teach and encourage every member to participate in the organizations and activities sponsored by the Church for temporal and spiritual development.

"What is it we heard a little earlier tonight? Do not

mistake activity for achievement? Excellent counsel. Driving an empty pickup from home to home does not advance the cause of Christ." He closed the booklet, tucking it under his arm. "I would like to comment on whoever it is in this stake that home teaches Brother Wheeler's associate at the university, that talkative home teacher we just learned about." He smiled at Brother Wheeler back on the front row.

"I think your fellow faculty members in the psychology department would agree with me, Professor Wheeler, that with all of our struggles in carrying bags of rocks, the ability to talk about one's self to others is a sign of great inner strength and confidence—unless it is done excessively. If it is painful or annoying to others, then it becomes something else; then it displays some grave weaknesses of character.

"What is that old saying? 'They don't care how much you know until they know how much you care.' I reason that any of us can get credit for having horse sense simply by bridling our tongue. I further challenge that if this garrulous home teacher in our stake made a concerted effort to fulfill the thirteen fundamental responsibilities we have just reviewed, then he wouldn't have any time left to weary his families with empty, ego-centered prattling." The president brushed his hand across his forehead and added, "I am embarrassed to admit that we once had home teachers coming to my house who provoked my oldest son to say facetiously, 'Every time our home teachers come I get my excitement level lowered.' "

The president leafed through his booklet once again, pausing to read a few lines silently. Then he addressed the group.

"What we have on the page following the thirteen responsibilities is a long list—a potpourri, if you will—of virtually everything any home teacher might wish to consider doing. Some of these items were already identified in the earlier material. Just be patient with us. We wanted to compile the most comprehensive itemization possible.

"And you will note that it is far too long, too detailed for me to present it orally, but I would like you to glance at it, just run your eyes down it. And remember, this is a list from which a concerned home teacher may build strong, helpful relationships:"

112 Considerations for a Concerned Home Teacher

• Recognize that you were divinely called to hold a sacred and specific stewardship to watch over each family assigned you.

• Always remember that you officially represent your quorum leader, the bishop—and the Lord.

• You may watch over your families in a variety of ways:

1. Making personal visits to their home or apartment.
2. Communicating—as needed—by phone.
3. Sending written messages such as letters, notes, seasonal cards, and remembrances.
4. Counseling with others when they request it.
5. Introducing them around the ward or neighborhood appropriately.
6. Offering to look after their interests in their absence.
7. Sitting with them in meetings.
8. Creating social opportunities together with them.
9. Drawing them into the circle of your friends.
10. Remembering significant events, such as graduations, achievements, birthdays, awards, recognitions, and special occasions of gladness.
11. Doing little thoughtful things on other occasions.

12. Helping to arrange for their transportation.

13. Remembering that you are the liaison between family members and their auxiliary and priesthood leaders, helping ensure their successful participation and involvement in Church programs. Who in the ward should know more about the needs of your families than you?

14. Knowing the Relief Society visiting teachers who visit the home and work with the family. They too are working toward common objectives with you.

15. Thinking about your families frequently during the month, their needs, their goals, and how you can help them.

16. Visiting when members are ill or bereaved.

17. Sending an occasional note or card to family members living away from home on missions, in the service, or away at school.

18. Greeting your assigned family members enthusiastically when you pass on the street or meet in the store. Go out of your way to extend heartfelt greetings and interest.

• Schedule a personal visit, sitting with them in their homes at least monthly.

1. Set this up in advance with each family. No surprises.

2. Make these arrangements at their convenience.

3. Let your family know your concern for them is genuine, not just to get credit for an end-of-the-month effort.

4. Bring an assigned companion, your assigned member of the Aaronic Priesthood or fellow quorum member. In certain circumstances, it is appropriate to take your wife as assigned by priesthood leaders.

5. Come with humility. You represent Jesus Christ.

• Plan and carry off successfully a monthly home visit.

1. Plan prayerfully with your companion for each monthly visit.

2. Block out a specific time to meet with your companion to plan what you will teach, set up your visiting goals, make assignments, etc.

3. Use the scriptures to teach your families, whenever possible.

4. Try to present a specific teaching subject each visit, one that will have general interest for the family.

5. Consider teaching the monthly message from the First Presidency found at the beginning of every *Ensign* magazine.

6. Be careful not to pontificate, preach, or talk only of yourselves, your ideas.

7. Remember that your personal testimony of gospel principles is the vital capstone in building relationships of trust.

8. Allow for your companion's participation. If he is young this will call for special tenderness and training.

9. Your visit should be structured—have a beginning, an ending, a purpose to achieve, a goal to accomplish.

10. Enter the home with a totally uplifting attitude.

11. Smile. Be warm, happy, effusive in your greetings, showing pleasure at seeing them.

11. Be sensitive to a sudden change in their situation, for example, if they have just received unexpected guests, sickness, problems, etc. They would appreciate your cutting your visit short with a promise to visit another time. If they are having unforeseen difficulties, you should offer appropriate help.

12. Recognize and honor the head of the home, deferring to him or her throughout the meeting, in getting started, making assignments, appointing someone to pray, etc.

13. At least one prayer is appropriate if it is agree-

able with the head of the family. Usually this comes at the end of the visit and makes for a natural conclusion and exit.

14. Be careful not to ask someone to pray who will not be able to do it. Better still, ask the head of the home whom he or she wishes to pray. You and your companion could quickly volunteer if there is hesitancy from family members.

15. A family prayer is usually a kneeling prayer, but this may not be the family's preference. Counsel with the head of the home.

16. When home teachers pray, they should specifically ask the Lord to bless the home and family.

17. How long should the meeting be? As long as it is productive and agreeable to the family. A shorter meeting is more appreciated than a longer one.

18. You should deliver any messages from the quorum leadership or bishopric, including announcements of ward activities the family might be interested in. This is especially beneficial for shut-ins or if no family members attend church.

19. Don't confuse your calling with the Lord's requirement that parents teach their children the gospel in the home. You should supplement the parents' gospel instruction.

20. If you cannot keep the scheduled appointment for some reason, communicate this immediately to the family.

21. Sometimes your most important role will be to listen. This is especially true of your visits to older single adults. They may be lonely. Your visit gives them a wonderful opportunity just to talk. What they think and feel should be of prime importance to you in your stewardship.

22. Use the missionary discussions—or portions of them—as basic teaching material.

• Know individual family members—their activities, progress, and special needs. Use that information to help them.

1. During your first visits, you might write down such vital information as names and birth dates—background information that would help you build your relationship with the family and as you communicate with appropriate priesthood leaders about their needs.

2. Inquire, when appropriate and after building a relationship of trust, about temple ordinances. If these have been neglected, encourage their completion.

3. Counsel parents in making sure all ordinances have been performed at the proper times, such as blessings, baptisms, and ordinations.

4. Invite family members to participate in the appropriate auxiliary organizations. If they are not doing so, convey this information to your quorum leader who will follow through in the Ward Correlation Council.

5. Act as a liaison, carrying back and forth between priesthood and auxiliary leaders and the family members any information that will help the family participate in the programs of the Church.

6. Some information from the family will be sensitive. You must carefully guard the privacy of those you are helping.

7. Counsel with the head of the home about special needs, feelings, failings, misunderstandings, and hopes of family members. Give your counsel prayerfully.

8. Share privileged information with other ward leaders only with specific permission of the person who confided in you.

9. Sometimes you may be informed of difficulties you cannot correct. For example, only the bishop can judge the worthiness of ward members. On such serious matters, you should stop being counselor and confidant, immediately suggesting setting up an appointment with the bishop.

10. Call all family members by their names, ex-

pressing special interest in each person, down to the youngest. Each is important to the Lord; you represent him.

11. Asking appropriate questions, especially early in your relationship as home teacher, unlocks the floodgate of wholesome communications. Be careful, however, not to be prying, inquiring about improper or personal things. But try to identify the major interests of each family member.

12. Counsel with the head of the home to learn the needs of family members.

13. Encourage the family to set up spiritual and temporal goals—as a unit—and then help them to periodically measure their progress and success.

14. Learn from the family what lessons they would like you to bring into their home.

15. Recognize the wishes of the head of the home in all matters. Respect the patriarchal principle that the father, or mother as a single parent, has the responsibility for individual and family progress.

16. Never come between a child and a parent.

17. Never gossip about the family.

18. Always be uplifting and edifying when discussing the family with appropriate Church leaders. Your report should have a singular goal: helping perfect the Saints, specifically this individual or family.

19. Let your family know you expect them to call you first if someone is sick and the elders are needed to administer. You should be the one to report this to your quorum leader, and he should report it to the bishop.

20. Be aware of any disabilities or chronic illnesses in the family.

21. Be aware of the family's general economic condition.

22. Know the family's major goals, interests, and worries.

23. Help your own family members to come to know your home teaching families so that there can be a unified and potentially effective family-to-family relationship.

24. Make yourself so close to and appreciated by the family that they think of you when priesthood support is needed. They will want to invite you into those special ordinances when blessings are given. You will become important to their family.

• Be a continuing source of encouragement to your families.

1. Encourage them to pray, individually and as a family.
2. Encourage them to study the scriptures daily.
3. Encourage them to hold family home evening.
4. Encourage them to become involved in writing personal and family histories.
5. Encourage them to do genealogy work.
6. Encourage the young men and boys to plan on a mission. Every young man who qualifies should become a missionary. Many young women desire to serve as missionaries. Older couples may be encouraged to consider a call as missionaries. You are in a position to reassure potential missionaries of the joy of serving the Lord in the mission field.
7. Encourage adult family members to attend the temple regularly.
8. Encourage the family to select and invite someone—nonmember friends, neighbors, classmates, coworkers—to hear the gospel in their home.
9. Encourage the family to observe the fast and instruct them in the merits of contributing to the fast-offering fund.
10. Encourage the family to take up a project of their choice where they can make some essential sacrifice to benefit others, enjoying the fruits of compassionate service.

11. Encourage the family to support the programs of the Church, including attendance at sacrament and other meetings.

12. Teach the family the importance of the sacrament.

13. Teach the family the importance of the atonement.

14. Discuss and work at building a testimony of Christ, of Joseph Smith, of our present prophet.

15. Discuss the magnifying of callings held by family members.

16. Discuss the meaning of being Christlike and of giving Christlike service to others.

17. Discuss the value of the ordinances of the gospel.

18. Discuss the value of paying tithing. (But it is not your province to inquire if family members pay tithing. That is the special domain of the bishop.)

19. Encourage the family to live the Word of Wisdom. (Direct questions on this subject are also the exclusive province of the bishop.)

• Help your families to become self-reliant.

1. If they need welfare assistance from the bishop, you should recognize this and notify your quorum leader or bishop.

2. Teach personal and family preparedness for emergency circumstances.

3. Encourage and teach your family to be financially self-reliant, such as avoiding debt, etc. (Do this without prying into the family's financial matters.)

4. Encourage your family to have a plan for physical fitness.

5. Encourage your family to use gospel principles in coping with the social, moral, and emotional challenges of today's world.

• Challenge your families to progress.

1. These challenges are invitations to become stronger in specified gospel areas where present weakness is recognized.

2. Challenges may be subtle, passive, implied, or quite forceful—as spiritually directed.

3. Challenges should not be so difficult as to discourage, not so simple as to fail to elicit a response.

4. Challenges should be worthy, appealing, specific, achievable.

5. The best challenge has a time schedule affixed.

6. Avoid blanket challenges, those given to the entire family, if you think they will retard individual action. On the other hand, a challenge for the family to pray together or attend church together has great merit.

7. All challenges should have doctrinal substance. You are asking the person to do what the Lord has specified for all his children to do in keeping his commandments.

8. Always show the benefits in meeting the challenge.

9. Once the challenge is given and accepted, build upon the person's desire to fulfill it.

• Make your companionship an example of service and concern worthy of the Savior himself.

1. Be available at any time.

2. The family should call you rather than the bishop for most needs.

• Ponder and pray over your families' needs.

• Earn the trust of your families.

1. They should believe in you and trust you as they would the bishop.

2. In all of your dealings, emulate qualities the Savior has taught us.

3. Remember that your families measure you in your integrity, truthfulness, attitudes, sincerity, and so on.

• Have a satisfying and motivating evaluation meeting at least monthly with your priesthood leader.

The stake president had allowed only a few minutes for the priesthood leaders to examine the lengthy list. But even as they became absorbed in the scanning, he broke into their concentration.

"Brethren!" He raised his voice above the growing groundswell of whispered comments. "Forgive me for moving us along, for this is an important list. It is so important that I want you to carry it home, carry it into your quorums, review it, study it, pray about it, ponder it. And let me suggest that it is not a laundry list of things home teachers *should* do. It is a poignant, powerful, refined inventory of things home teachers *could* do! Brother Wheeler has already cautioned the committee that lists might make people feel guilty. That isn't our intention. Our singular caution is this: no one can possibly do all of these things. But we should be familiar with them and consider them as ideas, suggestions. We may see where some item might genuinely help us improve our performance."

When their stake president became intense, his face colored, reddened. It was a ruddy pink now.

"I strongly suspect no one here among us has articulated even the majority of listed actions. But who here is not willing to try to do more? try to improve? This is the work of the Lord. This is as important as missionary work or temple work. This is the work of perfecting the Saints.

"And did you notice how many times we read key words like 'encourage,' 'persuade,' 'discuss'?

"There are over one hundred items listed here, with enough substance to them that no home teacher who studied and attempted to work that list should ever have to drive around 'empty.' " Then he offered as an afterthought, "And I'm sure all of you could add even more to the list with your collective experience."

The president cast about him, with a seeming loss of words. "During these past few weeks," he said finally, lowering his voice, "I have become overwhelmed with the incredible sweep and scope of the home teacher's duty and responsibilities. Gathering together this amalgam of all the Lord has commanded us regarding home teaching—commanded us in the scriptures and through inspired priesthood leaders—has stirred something deep within me. Looking back over the years, I realize now that I could have been much more helpful to families I home taught, and, sad to say, home teachers I directed.

"But we still have some chestnuts to roast," he said brightly. "Let me lead you rapidly through the final pages. They are as indispensable and as valid, in my judgment, as the materials just presented."

Notes

1. Marion G. Romney, *Conference Report,* April 1966.
2. D&C 107:99.

9

Summing Up for Serious Home Teachers

"That certainly is a long itemization of ideas for home teachers," the stake president remarked as he prepared to launch into the final pages of the booklet. "Surely you can use at least one of them on your very next visit. Try it! Select one and apply it right away. Then identify needs that others might fill from time to time. I promise that you will find yourselves actually looking forward to your home teaching work. And work it is! The Lord's 'work and glory.'

"But what of those who want no gospel conversation in their homes? 'You can come, but don't preach to me and don't try to get my kids to come to church. And if you try to pray like those last two who came, you'll find yourselves unwelcome here,' they say. All of you know the soft, caring approach of friendship and concern neighbors want to give each other. Try to establish a relationship of trust and perhaps someday, even years hence, they will respond. But they will have to feel a need before that will happen. Who knows when a crisis will occur that will send them right into your lives? The important thing is that the relationship already exists and they know they can call on you because you care about them. And maybe you are the only people they know in the Church. Be there for them!"

The president continued to clarify his feelings about the previous presentation. "I don't know if I agree with everything Brother Wheeler claimed about humor. I believe the scriptural cautions about light-mindedness. And I suspect he's right about humor being negative. But it would be a long day indeed if we couldn't see a lot in our lives to laugh about—especially if it only meant making fun of ourselves.

"General Authorities have lifted up our spirits with appropriate humor. I recall President Gordon B. Hinckley's rushing from the airport to a huge stake fireside some years back. He apologized for having such a tight time schedule, and then he said it reminded him of the man driving down a country lane who just had to stop his car when he noticed a farmer with a huge pig in his arms, holding it up to eat ripe apples off a tree. 'Isn't that time-consuming?' the incredulous man inquired. 'Sure,' answered the farmer, 'but what's time to a pig?'

"A recent Church historian, having carefully researched the life of Joseph Smith, wrote these words: 'The Prophet recognized as unhealthy the mind which lacked balance, perspective, and humor.'[1] And I have a similar quotation from Elder Boyd K. Packer, who said, 'A good sense of humor is a characteristic of a well-balanced person.'[2] I agree, brethren, that we must be extremely careful when using humor to teach the gospel in the homes of the Saints. But the right kind of humor could certainly warm them up to listen."

The stake president was well established and appreciated for his humor. "I saw a delightful bumper sticker this week that said, 'Trust Allah, but tie up your camel.' I suppose, Brother Wheeler, only camels would be offended at that one. On the other hand, someone this very evening asked me, 'How many home teachers does it take to change a light bulb?' And I just dreaded learning the answer: 'It takes only two, but they won't come till the last day of the month.'

"When I was bishop of the Third Ward, we were working on a massive reassessment of our home teachers, attempting to match up strengths with weaknesses, that is, placing strong home teachers with weak, needful families, and assigning weak home teachers to strong, active families. As we reviewed all those names, it became apparent that one of our sticky difficulties was in deciding, on the one hand, where to place those few brethren who didn't even want to home teach, while on the other hand figuring out who we would assign to those very few families who didn't really want home teachers.

"When someone finally said, 'Let's give them to each other,' we all laughed uproariously. It wasn't really that funny, but I suppose humor is more infectious late at night. And we were very tired." Now the president's broad smile faded to a thoughtful frown. He shook his head.

"Joking around that night provoked someone else to tell us still another humorous story—as he supposed—with home teaching as the focus of his joke. He described, very light-heartedly, as I recall, a creative pair of home teachers in our ward who had just established a unique visiting schedule: they waited till the last day of the month to home teach and then visited their same families again the very next day, which was the first day of the following month. That way, he explained to us, laughing as he told it, they got sixty days without having to make a visit."

The president's frown lengthened into a scowl. No one moved.

"As a case in point," he said in a stern voice, "after his humor fell flat, we looked up the several families those foolish home teachers were assigned. There were three families, and as their bishop I knew that each family had significant needs, one of them being their three inactive teenagers. None of those families would have been able to see and appreciate the insensitive humor of being visited every sixty days, two days in a row. What nonsense! What a commitment to foolishness! And all being done by the priesthood—and in the name of the Lord.

"No, my brethren, home teaching is the Lord's way of encouraging us to help each other, to deal with people's lives, with their faith, their hopes, their doubts, their needs. That is serious, solemn stuff." He gestured with a sweep of his arm. "You returned missionaries out there, did you ever attempt a door approach with humor, introducing yourself and your companion at some stranger's door with jests or jokes? No, no. Missionary work is also holy and of the Lord. Home teaching is a sacred calling. It is a sanctified trust."

He opened the booklet in his hand.

"One of the most significant scriptures printed in your booklet is on page 15. Let me read it to you: 'As ye are agents, ye are on the Lord's errand; and whatever ye do according to the will of the Lord is the Lord's business.'[3]

"Many of our home teachers don't recognize the seriousness of their assignments or the astonishing influence they might have, but are failing to achieve. Let me share with you several illustrations.

"As a bishop, I heard that one of our young couples was moving out of their apartment. I went to see them, to see if the ward could help them in the moving, to say farewell, to say I was sorry they hadn't been more active in the year they'd lived among us and could have enjoyed fellowshipping with the truly fine members we have in the Third Ward.

"The husband was very sour during my visit. He didn't rise to shake my hand but just sat staring at the floor. But the wife was quite talkative and animated. She admitted they were moving because—and I was caught off balance hearing this for the first time—they had decided to get a divorce. As all you bishops out there can well imagine, I immediately pulled on my marriage counselor's hat and tried carefully to get her (and him) to rehearse with me their problems. But she stopped me cold.

" 'No, no, bishop,' she said firmly, 'it's much too late for a reconciliation. We've both hired attorneys. The die is cast. We've divided up the furniture. We are not going back.' No amount of reasoning on my part could even get her to let me examine their expiring marriage. It was over. So then my pleadings turned into a lament. 'Oh,' I said, 'if only I had known sooner. If only you had told me your troubles earlier—'

"But she cut me off right there. She snapped back with considerable harshness, saying that she had revealed many months ago the threatening trend their marriage was taking. She had poured out her heart to the home teachers one dark night. Told them everything. And she fully expected that they would come tell me and that I would show up and start the healing process between her and her husband.

" 'Your home teachers,' I complained. 'They never told me, not a word.'

" 'Not *my* home teachers,' she corrected me bitterly. 'Those were *your* home teachers! I always thought home teachers represented the bishop. I thought that what I told them would certainly get back to you. And I spent many nights, many weeks, crying and waiting for you to call, to come. And when you never did, I just gave up. I only had the raw courage to tell that awful story just once. That was months ago. If only you had come then maybe we might have turned this mess around,' she said glancing over at her silent husband. 'But not now. It's too late now.' She was adamant about that."

The president shook his head in remembered disappointment and frustration.

"I felt so bad after hearing all that, the wife so cynical, the husband staring sadly at the floor. Nothing could be done. So I left. But I resolved to confront her home teachers.

And I did. I called them into the bishop's office, and we reviewed that plaintive night she had described to me. When she saw them last, they were hurrying off, out into the night. And they had never returned in the months since.

" 'Why didn't you come see me? tell me?' I asked them both, and believe me, this was a genuine, hard-as-nails reproach from their bishop, provoked by the Spirit. I was really put out. They were both elders, both active, responsive, bright and helpful in the ward. But both sat there looking at each other and down at the floor much like the failed husband the night before. 'What were you thinking of when she confided to you the desperate situation in her marriage?' I asked them. 'What were you going to do with this terrible message she'd just revealed? She opened her heart and soul to you two. What on earth were you both thinking of when you left her?' "

The president waited for this question to sink in.

"One of them finally got the courage to speak up and answer my question. 'Well, bishop,' he said lamely, 'actually we were both so embarrassed for her, for what she had told us, that we didn't tell anyone. And we never did have the heart to go back again. It was such a bad visit, such an ugly situation.'

"They were embarrassed!" the president protested. "Did you hear that? They were on this sacred assignment, they had a high and holy calling to represent the quorum president, their bishop, and the Lord himself—and they were embarrassed!" The president gritted his teeth, waved a fist over his head. "And what did I say to the two of them? I told them that I was embarrassed, monstrously embarrassed—for them! I was embarrassed that they were so selfish as to think only of themselves, their unpleasantness, their bad visit. An ugly situation, they had called it. But I called it their weak-willed dereliction of duty to the Lord and that miserable couple.

"I am rarely so spiritually upset with anyone as I was with those two negligent home teachers that night in my office. Talk about bad nights." The president's face had reddened up again.

"But I calmed down. We talked it out. I made sure they felt an increase in my love for them—just as the scripture we have referred to earlier counsels us.[4]

"We ended with a kneeling prayer together, and by the time they left my office, they had made a joint decision to hurry over to that gloomy couple and offer to do anything possible to help them both move out in their differing directions. You see, it finally occurred to them they had never been released. They were still home teachers—assigned to a family needing help."

The stake president glanced over at Brother Larrabee.

"That example, like the touching story told us about the weeping wife who had lost her sister and baby, illustrates again the profound weakness of some home teachers to communicate vital information properly. We can't hear often enough how important it is to communicate important messages.

"Now let us turn our attention to still another vital subject: time. Home teachers must make a sacrifice of their time to fulfill their stewardship. I remember a cartoon of a guard standing on duty in front of the Louvre—the celebrated international art gallery in Paris. An American couple are rushing up to him hand in hand, and the husband shouts, 'Quick, where is the Mona Lisa? We're double parked.'

"Some people home teach that way, in a 'honk and wave' kind of approach to their calling. President Benson once recalled, in a conference address on home teaching, a story President Marion G. Romney used to tell. A so-called home teacher called at the Romney home on a cold night. He kept his hat in his hand and shifted nervously when invited in to give his message, but he said he wouldn't come in. His message at the door was that it was so cold he had left his car engine running so it wouldn't stop. Then he added: 'I just stopped in so I could tell the bishop I made my calls.'[5]

"Dear brethren, what a vague, hollow visit. Home teaching should express love, compassion. True compassion is spontaneous; it doesn't wait till the end of the month to be expressed. And yet—" and the president exhaled a long audible breath, as in sorrow, "—at least he made this fumbling effort to contact his assigned family, and on a very cold night.

"But listen to this indictment against home teaching—the way we've been doing it—from an apostle who was trained as an attorney and learned to use words with real steel in them. This is from the late Elder Bruce R. McConkie, who minced no words when he said, 'Without question the greatest defect of the home teaching system in the Church is that it remains almost unused.'[6]

He looked fondly down at the booklet. "And that is what we hope this brief booklet might help us do, to learn to use more of the power in the Lord's program." He cleared his throat and raised his voice.

"Before we finish with these final pages, let me share two classic stories of effective home teachers. The first happened in our own Eighth Ward. Some of you are familiar with it. It is a simple story. The home teachers there discovered a brother who had been hurt in an accident at the neighborhood gas station he owned and ran. He had no insurance. He had heavy payments to the bank that he managed to keep up only as he ran the station.

"While he was worrying about finances, lying in the hospital on his bed of pain, his home teachers were the first visitors there to give him a blessing—two members of his elders quorum. They knew his business would be in jeopardy, so they also asked what could be done to keep it going. He and his wife had been beside themselves with grief and worry. The faithful home teachers promised that they would find some solutions. And they did.

"They reported his plight to their quorum presidency immediately. In this emergency, quorum volunteers were rushed over to keep the station open. On Sunday, the entire quorum voted to take turns running the business until their sick brother was on his feet again. The quorum also decided that as long as they were running the station, they might as well purchase all their gas and oil there. They circulated that plan to the high priests quorum and the Relief Society. The whole ward got behind the home teachers' inspired project.

"Though many of you know about that quorum project—and even supported it—few of you know how deeply it touched the entire family of the ailing elder. He hadn't been to church for years. But as he lay in the hospital getting day-to-day reports on this booming new business, he began to think about his life. His most frequent visitors were the two persistent home teachers. They were following through on their exciting quorum project, keeping him informed, cheering him up, giving him courage, expressing their fellowship—teaching him faith.

"He is on his feet now, active in a very successful business, active in the Church, active as a father and husband. May I share with you a touching and penetrating statement he made to me the other night as I countersigned his first temple recommend? He put it this way: 'Gratitude is a great eye-opener.' "

The president reached into his breast pocket and drew out a letter, which he unfolded.

"After setting up this ad hoc committee to improve our

home teaching, I phoned one of the great leaders in the Church and asked if he would put down on paper the testimony on home teaching I heard him bear years ago to a room full of prospective elders and their wives. He is a business and community leader, a stake president, and has chaired a major committee for the Church. But in the beginning, he was totally inactive." The president adjusted his glasses and read:

How Being Even a Reluctant Home Teacher Changed My Life

I have written my home teaching story out as simply as I could—and once more have experienced those feelings I had at the time I came into Church activity. Like many others I have been a reluctant home teacher. I was, that is, until a change came into my life.

I had recently come into activity after being many years outside the influence of the Church. The bishop assigned me as a senior home teacher with my returned missionary companion as the junior member. (The bishop was working on me psychologically.) We were assigned to two families where I could do little damage. A sweet widow lady said one night, "Why don't you call on the young family in the old rented house behind us. I believe they are members of the Church." I replied that we would report this to the bishop because we hadn't been assigned. We did report it to the bishop, who then said, "Why don't you call on this family?" And then we had no excuse.

The first night we visited this young family, there was a row of empty beer bottles on the front porch, and I thought, "Now, there's a man I can relate to." Timidly we knocked on the door. We could hear a baby crying in the background. The girl who answered the door was sixteen years old and very pregnant. The crying in the background was from a very sick baby. The young mother had swollen eyes as if she had been crying. She invited us in and told us that she would have to continue ironing a huge stack of clothes while we were there, and so we fumbled a great deal in our conversation in the visit and left after about fifteen minutes, telling her, "The Lord loves you." A few days later, my wife, Geneva, took a complete meal to them.

The next month, our visit was almost a repeat of that first occasion. It was near the end of the month. Again, the baby was crying in the background, and the young mother was getting closer to delivery. Again, she had been crying. After floundering a bit to make conversation and asking how we could help her, when it was obvious what we might have done, we left. And I went home rather indignantly. I said to my wife, "Why does the Church have a home teaching program that requires us to inflict ourselves on other people? Why isn't it set up so that the families can call us if they need us?"

Geneva said, "I think you'd better pray about it." I did pray, but somewhat belligerently.

The following Sunday was Fast Sunday. (You see how it works out, home teaching the last day of the month?) And I had promised Geneva I would try to give a name and blessing to our new baby. I determined I would sit on the front row so that I wouldn't carry a crying baby all the way up from the audience. Then, when I was called upon, I would merely stand in the circle and get the job done and sit down. Once I struggled through the procedure, I realized I was trapped. There was no way I could leave the meeting from the front row. I hadn't attended a testimony meeting for at least twenty years.

Near the end of the meeting, in a row near the back, a young girl stood up. I recognized her voice because of the tears in it. She said, "I've come to this testimony meeting to thank my Heavenly Father. We've lived in a home that we can't afford, and so

> we're moving. My husband is working two jobs, and I'm concerned about some of his other activities that are endangering our marriage. I came from a small town in Southern Utah and was married way too early. Our baby seems to have always been sick, and as you can see, it won't be long before we'll have another one. Twice in our marriage I was so discouraged I felt that I couldn't go on and would have to do something drastic with myself and my children. Each time I felt this way, I prayed as hard as I could—and each time our Heavenly Father sent the home teachers. I got past the desperate moments so that I could go on. I came here to thank my Heavenly Father for sending the home teachers."
>
> This young mother had received an answer to her prayers—and I had an answer to mine. That's why I believe in the home teaching program of the Lord.
>
> P.S. When the young family moved, my partner and I found their new address and, with the help of our bishop, called their new bishop and Relief Society president so there would be a follow-up for help.[7]

"Even a reluctant home teacher," said the president in a soft voice, "can be a marvelous tool in the hands of the Lord." He turned slowly through the final pages in his booklet and announced: "Page 16 now. I will simply read right through these, brethren, but you have them to take home, to study, to weigh, and to read again and again."

Melchizedek Responsibility to Aaronic Priesthood

> Melchizedek Priesthood bearers, when you have an Aaronic Priesthood young man as your companion, train him well. Use him effectively in working with your families and in teaching them. Have these young men feel of your love of home teaching so that when

they become senior companions, they will love their callings and magnify them as you have.

President Ezra Taft Benson
General Conference, April 4, 1987

Eight Ways to Support Your Aaronic Priesthood Companion

1. Plan every home teaching visit together.
2. Assign your companion to prepare and deliver a short inspirational thought, or to read and review a helpful scripture.
3. Include him in discussions held with the family being taught. Ask his opinion. Encourage his participation.
4. Help him learn how to contact families to make the appointments.
5. Plan visits at a time convenient to him as well as the family. If he can't go at a certain time, try to rearrange the schedule before attempting to get a substitute companion.
6. Counsel with him regarding specific things that could be done to help the family, such as shoveling a single mother's snow in winter, helping with yard work in the summer, and so on.
7. Get to know him. Encourage him in all aspects of his life. Make sure he knows you are his friend.
8. Remember he will be a missionary one day, spending much time in the homes of strangers. You can help him understand the power he has in bringing the blessings of the priesthood and the gospel into the homes of those he visits.

Counsel from the Prophet About Preparation

Home teachers should have a purpose or goal in mind and should plan each visit to help meet that purpose. Before making their visits, home teaching partners should meet together to pray, to review instructions from their leaders, to go over the message they will take to the families, and to discuss any special needs.

Home teachers should present an important message that they have prepared or that they bring from priesthood leaders. We strongly recommend that the home teachers use the monthly message from the First Presidency printed in the *Ensign* and the Church's international magazines. The head of the family may also request a special message for family members.

President Ezra Taft Benson
General Conference, April 4, 1987

Home Teaching Is the Basic Priesthood Activity

The significance of priesthood home teaching as it relates to the priesthood programs might best be illustrated as you answer these questions:

1. Can a member of the Church participate in missionary activities without holding the priesthood? The answer, of course, is yes.

2. Can a member of the Church participate in welfare-oriented activities without holding the priesthood? The answer, of course, is yes.

3. Can a member of the Church participate in genealogical activities without holding the priesthood? The answer, of course, is yes.

But concerning priesthood home teaching, only those who hold the priesthood are called to perform this activity.

Boyd K. Packer
Regional Representatives Seminar, October 2, 1968

The Biggest Hindrance to Home Teachers Is Procrastination

For behold, this life is the time for men to prepare to meet God; yea, behold the day of this life is the day for men to perform their labors . . . I beseech of you that ye do not procrastinate the day of your repentance until the end.

Alma 34:32–33

Making Friends of Your Home Teaching Families

To perform fully our duty as home teachers we should be continually aware of the attitudes, the activities and interests, the problems, the employment, the health, the happiness, the plans and purposes, the physical, temporal, and spiritual needs and circumstances of everyone — of every child, every youth, and every adult in the homes and families who have been placed in our trust and care as bearers of the Priesthood and as representatives of the Bishop.

President David O. McKay
Priesthood Home Teaching Handbook

Home Teaching Is Highly Valued by Church Leaders

I feel impressed to speak to you about a priesthood program that has been inspired from its inception, a program that touches hearts, that changes lives, and that saves souls; a program that has the stamp of approval of our Father in Heaven; a program so vital that, if faithfully followed, it will help to spiritually renew the Church and exalt its individual members and families. I am speaking about priesthood home teaching. . . . It is the priesthood way of watching over the Saints and accomplishing the mission of the Church. Home teaching is not just an assignment. It is a sacred calling.

President Ezra Taft Benson
General Conference, April 4, 1987

Home teaching is one of our most urgent and most rewarding opportunities to nurture and inspire, to counsel and direct our Father's children. . . . It is a divine service, a divine call. It is our duty as Home Teachers to carry the divine spirit into every home and heart. To love the work and do our best will bring unbounded peace, joy, and satisfaction to a noble, dedicated teacher of God's children.

President David O. McKay
Quoted by President Marion G. Romney
General Conference, April 8, 1966

There is no work in the Church where there is opportunity for selfless service of greater importance than that of the home teaching work. The Lord will bless you in the assignment where you are serving in proportion to your dedication to your assignment.

President Hugh B. Brown
Church News, March 18, 1967

Home teaching is the pivot on which all other programs turn. Home teaching is not just another program. It relates to all the programs of the Church. The Lord put the responsibility of the home teaching program on the Priesthood.

President N. Eldon Tanner
Lesson 8, 1967 priesthood manual

Home teachers are divinely commissioned . . . called into service by their priesthood leader after he has consulted and agreed with the bishop; they are guided in that service by the home teaching program sponsored and directed by the General Authorities. . . . The service itself, however . . . originated in the mind of the Lord Himself and was revealed by Him.

President Marion G. Romney
General Conference, April 8, 1966

Home teachers are an essential part of the power line that transmits the mind and will of the Lord through the channels he has ordained to the family and the individual. If there is a break in this line . . . the Lord's people are denied the full blessings which a perfect organization would bring them.

Elder Bruce R. McConkie
Regional Representatives Seminar, April 1973

Home teaching isn't just one of the programs. . . . home teaching is the instrument by which we see to it, through the Priesthood, that every program in the Church is made available to parents and their children.

President Harold B. Lee
Priesthood Home Teaching Handbook

We expect to see the day . . . when every council of the priesthood . . . will understand its duty; will assume its own responsibility, will magnify its calling, and fill its place in the Church to the uttermost. . . . When that day shall come there will not be so much necessity for work that is now being done by the auxiliary organizations, because it will be done by the regular quorums of the priesthood.

President Joseph F. Smith
Priesthood Home Teaching Handbook

When you were called, bishop, you were given an extension of your family—several hundred souls—old and young, some responsive, some responsible, a few not quite so responsible . . . but all of them are individuals. . . . You must not lose sight of that. You are teamed up in a powerful way with Melchizedek Priesthood quorums. . . . You have under-shepherds, the home teachers.

Elder Boyd K. Packer
Regional Representatives Seminar, October 2, 1968

The most effective reactivation is always on a one-to-one basis, on a family-to-family basis. It is personal contacting. It is friendshipping. It is done by the home teachers! Use the home teachers to reactivate! There is no substitute for home teaching.

Elder Bruce R. McConkie
Regional Representatives Seminar, October 1974

It is right to have the home teacher carry his responsibility of looking after the welfare of each individual. Assignments can properly be made so that every man who holds authority, which comes by direct revelation, may recognize his ecclesiastical duties by exercising the authority which he holds. . . . God bless you and give you inspiration . . . that every individual will be brought to a consciousness of the priesthood which comes direct from the Son of God.

President David O. McKay
Improvement Era, July 1963, p. 580

In 1963 home teaching was introduced to the Church. This differed from ward teaching in that greater emphasis was placed on watching over the family, rather than just making a monthly visit. . . . The home teacher is to keep in touch with the families, to watch over them, to contact them in whatever manner necessary, in order to watch over them. We were told that home teaching is not just the one visit a month, but that home teaching is never done.

Elder James A. Cullimore
General Conference, October 8, 1972

You can't magnify your priesthood and reject your call to do home teaching.

President Marion G. Romney
Church News, April 22, 1967

The home is the basis of a righteous life, and no other instrumentality can take its place nor fulfill its essential functions. The problems of these difficult times cannot better be solved in any other place, by any other agency, by any other means, than by love and righteousness, and precept and example, and devotion to duty in the home. . . . No other success can compensate for failure in the home.

President David O. McKay
Church News, January 7, 1967

Priesthood home teaching is here to stay. . . . There isn't any other way. All other activities are helpful. Some of them vital. But all are only part solutions. The only solution that can succeed is the one that relates directly to the family. Home teachers are the ones authorized to work directly with the family.

Elder Boyd K. Packer
Regional Representatives Seminar, October 2, 1968

The priesthood home teacher must think in terms of the needs of the family, not just another home to visit. And when he can feel the needs of individuals and, in his heart, when he can love them and has a yearning to help, he can give courage to struggling souls as they try to climb homeward in these perilous times.

Elder Rex C. Reeve
Regional Representatives Seminar, December 12, 1970

They had come to the last page of the booklet. Their stake president held his finger in place and looked up, glancing about. "Brethren of this great stake, I hope you see the awesome responsibility we have as home teachers. We cannot possibly do all of the things suggested in this little booklet. But we can do better than we have done. This final page is very special, for we wished to end on the highest of notes. It involves the magnifying of our priesthood. I ask myself continually that question: Am I truly magnifying my priesthood?

"Let me tell you about magnification. I once saw a demonstration in Washington, D.C., of a great sunglass measuring three feet across. It was a gigantic magnifying glass that gathered in the rays of the sun and focused them on a single point a few feet away, making that spot of magnified sunshine so hot that it melted a steel plate as easily as a hot knife passes through warm butter. I was told that scientists have not been able to accurately calibrate this enormous magnification of sunshine because it melts their instruments." With his finger still on the final page he peered over his glasses.

"Just think of that, what power only three feet of pleasant sunshine can create—when magnified!

"But we're down to the end of our time. We've come to the end of this little booklet on home teaching, and as we read the final page I must give you my own definition of home teaching. It is people helping people—but under the influence of the Lord, being guided by the Spirit." His face was quite flushed now. "And I must also tell you this: that the gospel of Jesus Christ is overwhelmingly uplifting to me. It is positive! It is exciting! We have felt the spirit of it here tonight. And that is an infectious spirit, a spirit that catches, communicates, is communicable. That is remarkable!

"It is this grand spirit that we find printed in these final pages, concluding counsel from a member of the First Presidency living in our day, followed by the word of the Lord—his anchoring statement on priesthood:"

Magnify the Priesthood with Diligence and Enthusiasm

> We magnify our priesthood and enlarge our calling when we serve with diligence and enthusiasm in those responsibilities to which we are called. . . . I empha-

size the words, diligence and enthusiasm. The Lord needs men, both young and old, who will carry the banners of His kingdom with positive strength and determined purpose.

President Gordon B. Hinckley
Ensign, May 1989

The Oath and Covenant of the Priesthood of God

For whoso is faithful unto the obtaining these two priesthoods of which I [Christ] have spoken, and the magnifiying their calling, are sanctified by the Spirit unto the renewing of their bodies. They become the sons of Moses and of Aaron and the seed of Abraham, and the church and kingdom, and the elect of God. And also all they who receive this priesthood receive me, saith the Lord; for he that receiveth my servants receiveth me; and he that receiveth me receiveth my Father; and he that receiveth my Father receiveth my Father's kingdom; therefore all that my Father hath shall be given unto him. And this is according to the oath and covenant which belongeth to the priesthood. Therefore, all those who receive the priesthood, receive this oath and covenant of my Father, which he cannot break, neither can it be moved. But whoso breaketh this covenant after he hath received it, and altogether turneth therefrom, shall not have forgiveness of sins in this world nor in the world to come. (D&C 84:33–41.)

Notes

1. Leonard J. Arrington, *Speeches of the Year* (Provo UT: BYU Press, 1974), p. 294.
2. Boyd K. Packer, *Teach Ye Diligently* (Salt Lake City: Deseret Book Company, 1975), p. 210.
3. D&C 42:29.
4. D&C 121:43.
5. President Ezra Taft Benson, *Conference Report,* April 1987.
6. Bruce R. McConkie, Regional Representatives Seminar, October 1974.
7. Letter from President Keith C. Brown, September 27, 1988.

Index